for Fiona, with love and thanks,

Rose Dennar

A Story of Transformation

How grieving my brother's death brought gifts of healing and awakened me to our power to renew the world.

Rose Diamond

BALBOA.PRESS
A DIVISION OF HAY HOUSE

Balboa Press books may be ordered through booksellers or by contacting:

Balboa Press
A Division of Hay House
1663 Liberty Drive
Bloomington, IN 47403
www.balboapress.co.uk
UK TFN: 0800 0148647 (Toll Free inside the UK)
UK Local: (02) 0369 56325 (+44 20 3695 6325 from outside the UK)

Print information available on the last page.

ISBN: 978-1-9822-8828-0 (sc)
ISBN: 978-1-9822-8827-3 (e)

Library of Congress Control Number: 2024903459

Balboa Press rev. date: 02/28/2024

Contents

Appreciations

I loved this book; I believe it's a must-read account of dying and the grief process. I would share this as a first stop read for those who have lost a loved one; in fact, it's the only book about death that has this much feeling, support and insights that I am aware of (and I've reads lots of them). As a book about personal grief there is so much to gain here. And then, with the eyes of a visionary, Rose sees further and shows how grieving can open the door to a more whole and loving self, and how this in turn brings healing to our world. This book will shine a light for many people who are in despair, whether from personal loss or in the face of the heartbreaking mayhem in our world. Rose shares her heart; this is a precious experience to be part of.

Dawn Grace Kelly, Spiritual Teacher and Healer

Raw, moving and inspirational, Rose Diamond presents an evolutionary odyssey - from the personal to the existential grief of death and loss she seamlessly weaves a road map, a tool kit and a reference book to guide us on the sacred journey from our own dark night of the soul, through the alchemical process of transmuting our suffering into personal and collective growth, raising the resonance of our individual and collective consciousness and becoming an integral part of a whole new paradigm shift for humanity.

Maggie Holling, Near-death experiencer and transition guide; life-long explorer of science, spirituality and soul

As I began to read Rose's story, I found myself completely captivated and absorbed. It's as if I'm there with each word written as Rose so beautifully and sensitively describes her journey through grief. The ups and downs, the soul searching and pain. What's different about this book is the amount of depth and detail she's willing to share, which is honest and raw.

The work I've done with Rose has helped me to understand the process of grief, its complexities and my own fear of dying. I've discovered, through applying some of the exercises, that grief isn't just about losing a loved one or someone close. For me it's about all the little deaths I've discarded over the years as being irrelevant: my own deep regrets and disappointments of paths and opportunities not taken, and unexpressed longings; betrayal in a relationship and friendships lost that left me in a great deal of pain and sadness. And recently being diagnosed with a potentially life-threatening illness that I've been able to embrace without fear and now see as a gift.

Liz Sokoski, Chair of Art & Soul, an arts charity that supports people with their mental health. Film maker and Transformational Coach, exploring the human condition.

Rose has shown great courage and wisdom with her conscious and attentive analysis of her own grieving process. Her insights are precious and pertinent as she finds the way to renewal and transformation and this book will provide a valuable guide to others on a similar journey. Rose explores grief as a key element, not only of the transformative soul journey, but as part of the collective transformation of humanity as we strive to evolve. It takes a deeply diligent and persevering mindfulness to feel into the beauty, hope and power hidden in our personal and communal grief, and more so to find the harmony between them - but it is essential work. This book will help us on our way.

Abigail Cheverst, Transformative community practitioner and student of spirituality

This is an important and valuable book for our times, when so many have suffered loss and grief, not only of the lives of dear ones, but in the many changes in the way we live our lives. Rose Diamond has gone deeply into the experiences of grief, taking lessons from her own life and offering her perspective in order to assist others in the grieving processes.

Grief is inevitably and of its nature a challenge – even if it offers opportunities for growth and learning as Rose shows clearly. As a trained therapist and counsellor myself, and also coming from an editorial perspective and being practised in taking a detached critic's stance, since reading Rose's book I have found myself with recurring thoughts and revived memories to explore. Her advice to absorb the book in smaller instalments and take time, is important. I sense it will be a slow burn experience for many, and people will dip in, reflect, return, reassess and ultimately find the healing.

In describing the benefits for grieving well, Rose is solution focused and offers a means of finding relief, learning, raising awareness and finding inner peace, and release from sadness … these are the things that so many people are seeking in these times of loss, disruption and rapid change.

Christine Miller MA, author of the comprehensive global study of Love and caring at work, 'Love in the Boardroom'

A Story of Transformation is an engaging and stimulating combination of appropriate and moving personal disclosure and insights, information on loss, and gentle encouragement to explore the unchartered waters of one's personal grief journey. Rose offers a unique perspective and I'd recommend it to clients and friends who want to explore their loss at a deeper, more spiritual level. I was often moved to tears and reminded of my own similar journeying toward death with my dear friend and spiritual companion, as well as the parallel loss of my beloved mum, to whom I was unable to say goodbye.

Jan Cleghorn, Psychotherapist

I found myself nodding all through reading *A Story of Transformation*, partly at the common experiences of loss and grief, a recognition of not being alone in this. Also at the insights I received as Rose's particular skill of weaving her story alongside her years of professional experiences offered me new ways of looking at how I have responded in my own life. I have read many excellent books on death and grief, and I feel this will become a well-regarded classic alongside those. Highly recommended to anyone who would love to fully be with their own grief and be transformed by it, in the company of a wise guide.

Mary Lunnen, Writer and Life Coach

Rose Diamond skilfully and insightfully identifies the depth & complexities of loss in a clearly recognizable way. She paints familiar heartscapes, and the eloquence and fullness of her words unlocked my paralysed being as I picked up all the pieces of a shattered life, following the death of my son. She gave life and a voice to the death I feel inside. Rose writes in a wholeheartedly honest way sensitively reflecting a wealth of knowledge and personal experience. It is this deep, experiential perspective that connects me to my own experience of grief and loss and its expression.

A Story of Transformation provided an anchor, a lifeline like point of reference in the navigation of my shattered world and a reminder that the relentless journey of grief and loss can lead to growth and transformation if the process is allowed to unfold organically. Rose's work with grief, loss and transformation has helped fill a great void left by the pain & suffering of losing a child and enabled me to embrace life in a much more authentic way and to dare to feel hope again.

With gratitude and love, Margie Austin, Kinesiologist

This book for me is a story of transition. From an author who has been there. And one, who, like me has transitioned into a new life and consciousness. And the transition was painful.

My own experience of grief wasn't anything like I imagined it would be. After my dear husband died the words and actions of well-meaning friends and family caused me to doubt myself. When I read Rose's words "the chaotic experience of loss" something deep inside me responded with relief. Because I did feel his loss intensely and there is certainly chaos when someone close to you dies. Recently, I had begun to be concerned that perhaps I had not grieved properly; whatever that means. But Rose's book has put it all in place for me. And looking back on the last five years, I can see more clearly that my path has been a process of transformation in which finally I have learnt to choose life, live in gratitude and be a light in this chaotic world.

For me this book is enlightening and very thought provoking. I think readers would benefit more after the initial "Chaotic experience of loss" has calmed down somewhat. And suddenly one is left with "What now?"

Patricia Cherry, Author

Reading *A Story of Transformation* helped immensely from the perspective of having lived through the experience of the death of a loved one multiple times and being able to truly, intimately relate to Rose's words, story, experience and sharing. Rose has a gift with words and her sensitivity and transparency make the book a fresh current of lived experience which can only be authentically helpful. I absolutely recommend this book as I know it will help others on the journey of experiencing the death of a loved one and particularly being able to "normalise" this experience. Rose's wisdom is backed with integrity, a gentle presence and deep-felt interest and knowledge of the topics.

Pujari Dickson, From Womb to Tomb Guide

I am grateful for having read Rose Diamond's book, *A Story of Transformation*. Like Rose with her brother's death I went into a deep, dark night of the soul after my husband's death. It took me many years to walk out and into the sunlight again. During the time surrounding the death of my husband I lost my health, my massage business, my beautiful home in the mountains, and moved away from my friends and community to another state. I dove deep into my healing and transformation in the following years and have found joy in life again.

A Story of Transformation took me deeper still, it became so clear while reading it, and doing the practices and questions of inquiry, that the journey of transformation is never complete. This book showed me that where I still suffer is linked to the griefs in my life and gave me a "roadmap" of how to heal. There is suffering in our grief, sometimes excruciating pain for a long time, there is also beauty and a heart that can transform into deeper love and compassion. As we move through the chapters in our life, we can truly heal from all we live through, truly enjoy this life we are given, and then go on to help others. These were my thoughts when I closed the book.

Fran Purkey, Certified Massage and Energy Clearing Therapist

As soon as I sat down to read Rose's book, I knew I was going to receive so much information, a-ha moments, inspiration, resonance and understanding. I was right in that knowing. Beautifully written throughout, soul seekers everywhere can gain much wisdom from these pages. Rose takes the reader on a journey from approaching the death of a loved one, the transition time, the funeral, the grief journey, soul seeking and deep spiritual reflection including the dark night of the soul.

It's a journey I have been on so there was a value in these words that hugely resonated with me. I lost my brother when I was just 36 – he was 43 and died of leukaemia. It brought back fond memories of the experience – I say fond because, although it left me with emotional scars, I became a person more in tune with life and everything in it, as Rose describes very eloquently in her book. Rose's book will no doubt help to comfort, reassure and heart warm the reader and anyone going through a similar experience. It really is all about sitting with, and looking very intently at death, and choosing life.

Jackie Deakin – Soul Midwife and Life Celebrant

I found reading *A Story of Transformation* extremely moving as a truly honest heartfelt account of Rose Diamond's own many layered experiences of great grief. Some parts of her story resonated with my own feelings and I was particularly moved by the description of some of her brother's behaviourisms with which I could personally identify, giving me renewed recognition of my patterns and therefore a place for me to focus with my continuing inner work.

Casey Howse, Massage Therapist

I feel so moved and uplifted by Rose Diamond's writing. She is so open, revealing, insightful and honest, sometimes painfully so. This book touched me greatly and brought up feelings of my partner's dying and the bewilderment I struggled with afterwards. I feel such gratitude for Rose and her willingness to share so deeply. Thank you!

Siena Ammon, Artist

For David

and for all those who

have grieved the death of a sibling.

Prelude

This is a story of how new nourishing possibilities can be seeded in the darkest times and how grieving, healing and creating are woven together as three strands of a single braid that can be your lifeline through the dark.

Just after midnight on a quiet and sober New Year's Day, I stood above the beach in Pohara, Golden Bay, New Zealand, and declared my strongest wish for 2015: to visit my soul friend, Woods, in Virginia USA and then go on to stay with my brother David, in England.

I had lived in New Zealand, on and off, for twenty years. On that New Year's Day, it had been four and a half years since I'd last visited Woods and five years since I'd seen my brother. I had an empty space inside that could only be filled by the quality of relationship I had with Woods; even when we lived far apart our connection was deep, natural and mutually inspiring. I was also on a mission to help my brother move through his grief, following the death of his partner nine months previously, and then to pursue his dream of buying land in Wales and building an eco-home.

My lifestyle in New Zealand was rich in creative and spiritual freedom and low on dollars and I had no idea how I was going to bring my intention into reality by buying a ticket to the east coast of the USA, and then on to London. Yet, from that moment, with the New Year breeze on my face, I held the knowing that I would go. I named a date in April and, sure enough, at the end of April I was on my way.

I can't imagine how I would feel now if I hadn't made those visits. Those five precious weeks with Woods were the last time I saw him alive. I can see him now in my mind's eye, at the end of my stay, a lone man standing on the station platform smiling courageously as my train pulled away towards Washington. My sadness at saying goodbye to him was mixed with gratitude for our rich friendship and I was already looking forward to the next time I would see him.

But life doesn't always go according to plan and four months later he was diagnosed with lung cancer and told he had weeks to live. Just how many weeks we didn't know. We hoped there would be time to complete some creative work together but this was not to be. I wanted to go and take care of him in his last weeks but, for his own reasons he said no, and I could only respect his wishes, so we met several times a week online to say our goodbyes. Woods approached his death consciously, with grace, humour, caring and self-responsibility. He died on December 22nd, 2015.

I was living with my brother then and, soon after Wood's death, I took off from David's home near London to the foothills of Snowdonia in Wales, where I eased my grief by submerging myself in writing about Woods and his conscious dying process. I completed a book called *Portrait of a Gentle Man*.[1] Then I wrote another about the *Deep Discovery Conversations*[2] he and I had so much enjoyed. This concentrated focus supported me to sit with my feelings of grief and loss every day.

Six months later, as I was beginning to emerge from the intensity of grieving for Woods, my brother died suddenly. Once again, I embarked on the project of writing my way through my grief and pulling together the threads of my story as best I could.

Death Calls Us Out of Our Comfort Zones and Into the Unknown

A Story of Transformation began as a way to come to terms with David's sudden death and the stark reality of being the only member of my family still alive. On some days my brother's dying felt like a meaningless loss but, as I wrote, I became curious about grief – how we grieve, what happens when we don't and what motivates one person to undertake the work of conscious healing during their lifetime, while another doesn't. I have always loved writing and it's been one of my most valuable vehicles for healing and creativity through many troubled times. Now it gave me the opportunity to make space for my grief, to enter into it, walk around in it, feel it deeply, become familiar with it, explore all its contradictions and nuances, and move through it. At the same time, the presence and focus writing requires opened up a space for new possibilities and a chance to go beyond the pain of grief, to find the gifts within it and take my next step towards new life.

Just as writing offers a private space in which to delve and feel deeply, it also helped me to bring order and form into the chaotic experience of loss and to find some sort of completion and closure to this difficult passage in my life, and an integration within myself. Yet, although we humans need closure, so many things in life and death can't be neatly tidied away. Death calls us out of our comfort zones and invites us to sit with it, naked, eye to eye, to feel its power and presence. Grieving is a form of love, and like love and creative freedom, it is disorderly and won't be contained in any convenient boxes.

As I felt into my brother's life and death I came to realise just how much our culturally created avoidance of death and grief negatively impacts our individual and collective well-being and diminishes our creative power. My curiosity about this led me deeper into inquiry and I came to see my brother's story, although tragic from one point of view, as inspiring. At the age of 71, just before he died, he broke out of a lifetime's low self-esteem and creative disempowerment caused by an abusive childhood and followed his dream. Although I was devastated by his untimely death, the fact that he found the courage to make this breakthrough made him my hero.

A Story of Transformation

My initial grief for my brother's death was just the beginning. Nine months later I was dismayed to enter a second and deeper state of grief. This became a story of transformation, very personal and challenging, and at the same time it was a meeting with something much bigger than me, and potentially liberating. Over the next few years my personal grief at being the last remaining member of my family merged with a massive collective grief as our world descended deeper into the chaos and despair of the climate emergency, the extinction crisis, the pandemic, wars and genocide, mass migrations, and the impending collapse of the systems which maintain life. Within this maelstrom of change and destruction I experienced a descent into the inner shadowy realms of the psyche, an experience which has been described by many sages as the dark night of the soul.

There were times I met despair when everything I valued appeared to have been stripped away and I could find no comfort anywhere. I lost sight of my creativity, the part of myself I most treasured and which I had always relied upon to get me through hard times. Yet, as I summoned the courage to take each next step, I grew in strength. Not the apparent strength of putting on a happy face or pretending I didn't need anyone but a quiet resilience that embraces raw emotion and vulnerability.

As difficult as this descent into my own darkness was, I came to see a meeting with death as a special opportunity to move beyond the veils of habit, through deathliness and into new life. This meant leaving behind old ideas of who I am and how life works, and entering an unknown space in which I am a complete beginner, seeing anew, knowing anew.

Grief has taught me to live in the moment, here and now, and be willing to welcome all my emotions and feelings, no matter how painful or contradictory. As I practice being with whatever is arising in my experience in this way, eventually a new spaciousness opens up. It is within this space that the possibilities for new life can be gathered and the seeds that have been planted in the darkness begin to sprout into a tender trust in the process of life itself. From the composting of loss, grief and death, we can gather flowers of wholeness and harvest a deep gratitude for being alive.

As grief took me deeper into inquiry and stripped away layers of my outgrown identity it became a doorway into renewal. I was challenged with the choice:

Do I want to go on living or not?

When I realised yes I do, the next question arose:

Then how do I choose to live?

In response to these two crucial questions I made a conscious choice: if I am to be granted another chapter of life; if I still have things to do and people to touch and gifts to share; then I choose a fully embodied, purposeful and joy-filled life.

All around the world people are facing these questions every day as our world crumbles around us. For me, and for many people I know, making the choice to live wholeheartedly is just as testing as sitting with death.

In this book I explore how it has come about that so many of us have arrived at an ambivalent relationship with life and death. I show how, for those of you who want to resolve this ambivalence, maintaining a bigger perspective combined with simple daily practices, can support you through these very troubled times so that you can find your wholehearted YES to life.

I wrote the first draft of this book in 2016 as I was grieving for David. Then, my longing to connect with others looking for meaning and solace following some heart-felt bereavement or loss of their own, moved me to start sharing my writing. Convinced that grieving well can become a vital process of renewal, I brought groups together for deep discovery conversations to explore death, what happens to us after we die, and how we can make the journey through grief in a conscious way that fertilises our growth. These explorations had a life of their own and, in no time, I was creating a project in grief awareness which I called, *The Sitting with Death and Choosing Life Programme.*[3]

Through these unexpected developments in my life story I've discovered untold riches within the apparent tragedy of death and loss. I've seen more deeply into my own story and into the deeper meaning and purpose of life. I've realised the role I took on as a child as the family healer was not the burden I felt it to be but an opportunity to learn and grow, to find meaning and self-actualisation within suffering and to receive fulfilment through being of service. And more than that, I've discovered how death, as well as being a source of heartbreak, may also be a victory. I hope the personal stories of my brother's life and death, and my own, will touch your heart and become a means to discover your own meaning and motivation.

The movement through grief and loss to the conscious choice for fully lived life is a vital rite of passage that can transform each of us individually and renew our world. Death may appear to you in many forms: the loss of a loved one; facing mortality through your own aging or ill health; allowing yourself to deeply feel the impact of the ecological and humanitarian crises in our world; or suffering the falling away of an outgrown identity. However it comes, death invites us into a greater intimacy with the darker, shadow side of human nature – our own and that of our species. If we do not shy away, we may open more fully to the hidden gifts and mysteries of being human and willingly embrace our power to heal ourselves, our families and our world.

Rose Diamond,
December 2023

How to Get the Best from this Book

*"Be patient to all that is unresolved in your heart and try to love
the questions themselves like locked rooms, like books written in a
foreign tongue…What matters is to live everything. Live the questions
for now. Perhaps then, you will gradually, without noticing it, live
your way into the answers, one distant day in the future."*
Rainer Maria Rilke[1]

This is not a big book in terms of its number of pages but it is a book that
addresses big questions about death, grief, loss, healing, creativity and our
purpose for being here. What could be bigger than these themes in any
human life?

I recommend that you don't try to read the entire book in one sitting
or skim through it. Rather, I encourage you to take your time and to use
what I have written from my experience to feel into your own life and find
your own questions.

In this sense I invite you to participate in the book. Sit with those parts
of my story that touch you and notice what is stirred within you.

Your experiences will be different from mine but I'm sure there will be
common themes. The ways you understand the world will also be unique to
you. I am not asking you to agree with what I've written nor am I claiming
to know "The Truth". I do my best to express the truth of my experience
as clearly as I can and I encourage you to take whatever is inspiring to you
from my writing and use it to help you clarify your own experiences and
authentic truths.

To make this easier I have included questions for inquiry at the end of sections and some simple practices which will help you to develop your skills for moving through grief in a way that will nourish you.

Please grab your journal, make yourself comfortable and dive in.

Definitions

The theoretical underpinnings which guide my life, and which you will find in this book, are a synthesis of my life experience. Many authors and teachers have contributed to my understanding and I don't follow any one teaching. My philosophical and psycho-spiritual understandings are a constantly evolving conceptual map which supports me to find my way through challenging inner states towards wholeness. I am including these definitions here so that you will know how I am using these concepts throughout the book.

soul – a dimension of consciousness which carries our evolving individual story and a treasure trove of personal wisdom and gifts, along with our history, our karma, our potential and destiny.

Soul – a species Soul or Over Soul which carries our collective story, gifts, history, karma, potential and destiny.

In my experience, when I am open to receiving inspiration, both the individual soul and the species Soul may speak through me. This is an edge of understanding which I am currently exploring and it is not always easy to discern when the personal soul is at play and when it is the species Soul, or indeed, where one ends and the other begins. Please bear with me.

The Soul Journey – The individual and collective process of realising our wholeness by knowing ourselves as spiritual beings here on Earth to have a human experience and to bring the spiritual energy of soul into embodiment and harmony with life.

Soul Work – Our unique calling and set of gifts which motivate us to grow in wisdom by engaging with life, expressing ourselves authentically and taking action to offer our gifts.

Conscious Evolution – A term made popular by Barbara Marx Hubbard[2], and many others, exploring how, by being conscious of humanity's history and how things evolve, we can co-operate with and make an intentional effort to drive forward our individual and collective evolution. We can choose co-operation, co-creation and sustainable practices over self-destruction, separateness, competition, and ecological devastation.

Conscious Healing – An integral, whole-systems approach to healing based on the restoration of wholeness. Guided by the understanding that we are each part of an interconnected world and cosmos that includes physical, emotional, mental, spiritual and cultural dimensions, and the natural world, we can consciously choose to heal ourselves and participate in a transformational process which raises and expands consciousness and has positive effects across all dimensions.

The Evolutionary Impulse – a term coined by spiritual teacher Andrew Cohen[3] meaning an ecstatic drive to create the future: "a mysterious urge toward unbounded freedom and our own potential for radical transformation in this life." In my experience the evolutionary impulse is one form of inspiration which informs, directs and uplifts me.[3]

Transformation – the alchemical process by which the base metal of the conditioned mind, which separates, is turned into the gold of a more integrated consciousness, which makes whole and unifies. In psycho-spiritual terms, typically this means seeing through, letting go and deconstructing old ways of seeing and behaving, so that we can live more fully from the wisdom of the soul, embody that wisdom and bring it to Earth.

[4] Questions for Inquiry

Please see this book as an invitation into your own inquiry. Everything I have written is stimulus for your exploration. The questions for inquiry will help you to digest what you are reading and view your own experiences in the light of any new insights or perspectives.

Inquiry is a beautiful process because once you have clearly identified your questions, the answers will come. Perhaps you will pick up a book, or have a conversation with a friend, or you will remember a dream, or you may be walking in nature and suddenly the brilliance of insight will come alive within you. Don't expect to find your answers all at once but engage with the questions as a lived inquiry that accompanies you through your days.

[5] Practices

The practices I offer are very simple but changing lifelong patterns is not easy. If you only read the instructions, or do the practice once, nothing much will change. But if you value the practices as opportunities to release yourself from limited patterns and to transform your behaviour, and you take a short while every day to focus your awareness, you will gradually free yourself from the past and, in time, become more loving, more fulfilled and more empowered.

Access to Your Free Resources

You may prefer to listen to some of the practices and meditations and you will find recordings I have made for you on this webpage, https://www.tribeintransition.net/a-story-of-transformation-free-resources/ along with other free resources and ideas of how you can take the practices further.

Disclaimer

The information in this book is educational in nature. The questions for inquiry and the practices are experiential and cannot be relied upon as a means for self-healing. The stories throughout the book are personal experiences of healing and transformation and may stir any incomplete grief residing in the reader. Professional advice or support should be sought from a qualified health professional for any medical or mental health matters. The author accepts no responsibility or liability for the use or misuse of information or sources provided in this book or in any related materials.

Chapter One

Grieving

My Brother David

I flew from Washington to London Heathrow a few days before David's 70th birthday. He was half an hour late arriving to pick me up and, as I watched him approach, I immediately noticed how aged and overweight he was. A complex mix of shock, impatience, tenderness and resignation flooded through me. He looked eccentric and vulnerable, an aging Billy Bunter, with a big belly hanging over his shorts, no jacket, and his walk a kind of penguin waddle. The accumulated heartaches and neglects of a difficult life, filled with too many disappointments and compromises to his

1

creativity and self-esteem, had taken their toll and weighed heavily on him. I'd come from the other side of the world to support him to move beyond this sorry state and make the leap he was longing to make, to follow his passion and actualise his dream of buying a plot of land in Wales and to build an eco-friendly home there. At 70, this was his chance to make the break for a freedom that had eluded him so far. Aside from being his sister, I was a good person to accompany him on this adventure because my life for many years had been an uncompromising bid for creative sovereignty and I had learned a lot along the way; or so I thought.

I lived with David, on and off, for the next nine months before taking off for North Wales to grieve for Woods. We saw each other for the final time at Easter 2016, three months before he died. By then, he had bought a piece of land he loved in Pembrokeshire, West Wales, and was very close to selling his house in outer London. When he met me at the station, I saw the twinkle of love in his eyes instead of his former pain; the light of hope in place of despair.

The Death of a Family Member is a Special Opportunity

The work of grief is in allowing our humanity, in all its aspects, to move through us and to transform the heart.

It wasn't easy living with my brother and, when I think of him now, my strongest wish is that I had been kinder. My nomadic lifestyle in New Zealand had fostered a desire for a kind of zen-like simplicity and I found material clutter distracting. David lived out his days from the sofa in the living room within a fortress of assorted debris which he was always in the process of tidying; a task he never completed. The dining room was also stuffed to the brim with boxes gathered after our father's death. The only place we could sit, eat and relax together was in the messy living room.

When viewed from the perspective of life and death, the discomfort of living in a shambolic environment is trivial, yet it's the stuff we humans fuss and fight about. Such differences become accentuated when old family patterns are activated and I reacted to the mess with stress and exasperation.

David's inability to hear my pleas evoked in me an old familiar feeling from childhood of having no boundaries nor the right to define my own life. I asked him to tidy the living room, I told him how the mess affected me, I offered to do it for him, I sulked, I lost my temper. It took me several months to see how, while he was sitting behind a barrier of old papers, cardboard boxes, used plates, old socks and handkerchiefs, CDs, paper clips and magazines, I was sitting behind a barrier composed of my judgments. And it was my judgments that were making me miserable. As soon as I realised this I began to practice shifting my focus away from the disarray and irritation, and towards acceptance. I relaxed and that helped. It was a simple, powerful and humbling lesson in not taking things personally, or getting captured by limiting thoughts, while learning to accept otherness. These kind of lessons always lie latent within family dynamics and the grieving process is a wonderful opportunity to cleanse the dross away until only love is left.

With my judgments suspended I began to feel into my brother's experience of life with more empathy. I guessed the barricades David built around himself, with his big stomach, eccentric appearance and fortress of clutter, were his way to protect himself from intrusion. These lifelong habits, originated in childhood abuse, were a comfort zone constructed to keep people at bay. And behind the barricade was hidden this man, my brother, whom I really knew so little.

Anyone who has grown up through the trauma of an abusive childhood, or suffered at the hands of a bully, will know how difficult it can be to draw healthy boundaries throughout a lifetime. I've experienced this difficulty too; it has caused me a lot of distress and been a source of lifelong learning as I've slowly grown in self-awareness and learned how to say No clearly and Yes wholeheartedly. Within the abused person lives a malignant belief that we are not worthy to say no or to have our own needs met; we believe other peoples' needs are more important. Or, on the other hand, in our determination to get our share of whatever's going, we may trample roughshod over others. In any case, an easy flow of giving and receiving, is elusive for those who start life in a punitive atmosphere.

We each find our own ways to adapt and David had to contend with the impatience and aloof withdrawal which were my way of creating boundaries.

For instance, I preferred to be alone when cooking and I felt cramped and fussed over by his cheerful offers of help, so rather than welcoming his attempts at friendship, I banished him from the kitchen. This is a small unkindness in the scheme of things but, when the other person has gone and won't be coming back, regrets about such lost opportunities and little acts of meanness linger and create remorse. Sitting with remorse has been a part of the grieving process that helped me to see my old limiting patterns more clearly and eventually motivated new behaviours. Such lessons in self-awareness are intrinsic to the work of grief.

Despite our difficulties, this was an opportunity for us to get to know each other as brother and sister. I'm David's kid sister; he was there the day I was born, and he's always been there. He began life with a sunny nature and, in my favourite photo of him, he was six and I was two years old. I'm sitting on a tricycle and he's standing beside me bright and happy, a mischievous little boy. Mostly, he tolerated me although he'd much rather have been off fishing and doing boy things with his mates.

Ours was one of those families in which everyone was separated whilst at the same time being claustrophobically bonded together. Our father controlled through divide and rule, criticism and a foul temper. David got the worst of it and was constantly the focus of dad's rage. I was a suffering witness to the emotional and physical abuse to which our father resorted when frustrated and to the endless rows between our parents. Although he never hit me I listened as he struck both my mother and my brother and this filled me with fear and engendered a deep sense of injustice. David's self-esteem was badly damaged by the repeated explosions of dad's vitriolic disappointment, as was mine. I only realised many years later that my father didn't have to lay a hand on me in order for me to be traumatized. The vibrational impact of his rage on my energy body was violent in itself and shook me to the core. It was several years after dad died before I was finally able to find forgiveness and acceptance and to see how he too longed for connection yet didn't know how to connect. He was so caught in his own pain, frustrations and trauma, he drove away those whose love he longed for the most.

As teenagers, growing up in the '60's, David and I escaped from the oppressive environment of our home as best we could. With me on the back of his motorbike, we'd head off to Richmond or Windsor, on the outskirts of London, to see one of the many rock and blues bands transforming the cultural scene: John Mayall's Bluesbreakers, Georgie Fame, the Yardbirds, Big Bill Broonzy, Graham Bond. David had an encyclopaedic knowledge of rock band lineages and, when we sat together fifty years later in his chaotic living room, he would name every old rocker who came on the TV and recite all the bands they'd played in. I wasn't quite as enthusiastic as he was but we shared a heritage as rock n' roll mystics of the sixties, with rock music our medicine and stairway to heaven. When we arrived home from school, we'd compete to play our 45s and LPs on the family stereo; he'd play Dave Brubeck and Bob Dylan; I'd play Spencer Davis and the Beatles. Mum was in the kitchen cooking the evening meal and she never complained about hearing the same song for the hundredth time. Those were happy times for the three of us.

Our father also had a great love of music and found solace in it. He and David shared a wonder at the Universe and how it works; Dad was a mathematician and a geologist, David a physicist. But despite the fact they had much in common they never saw eye to eye or heart to heart. For dad, David was always a disappointment and he never let any opportunity go by to punish him for not living up to his expectations. That wounding shaped

David's character and life choices and he nursed these wounds until the day he died.

After our teenage years my brother and I didn't see each other much for a while. He married and had a regular job, an organic veggie garden in the country, and a son who became profoundly disabled as a result of an illness when he was a baby. Taking care of his son at home was a big challenge in David's life and it put so much strain on his marriage that a bitter divorce resulted in which he lost heavily emotionally and financially. The hurt of his son's disability and the divorce were now added to the wounds from our father's punitive control. I had moved to Scotland where I'd become a poet, a gestalt therapist and a change agent. I invited David to visit me two or three times in Edinburgh and then in the North-West Highlands of Scotland. He was always affable and good natured, a kind of bumbling innocent who meant well but didn't quite fit in his body or on the Earth. In company, he expressed a hearty optimism and enthusiasm which, to my ears, never rang true. With him, I felt the inner conflict which I experienced with all my family: an intense sensitivity to his suffering and a desire to help mixed with a powerlessness to know how to best provide support, played off against a desire to be free to get on with my own life. I was no expert at life or love myself and I channelled the pain of relationship conflicts into my work.

Even during this long period when we had chosen very different, even diametrically opposed life paths, occasionally David and I would take some time to be alone together and he'd put on some fabulous guitar riffs and pour a couple of glasses of fine malt whisky. Then we'd be back in rock and roll mystic freedom for a while, rocking out to the soul sounds of our generation, with their magic mix of cultural rebellion, longing for transcendence, raunchy sexuality and genius artistry.

Apart from having rock n' roll in common, we were both teachers, although David didn't start out that way. He began his working life in industry, and I remember when he came home from his first job and talked about the massive machine he was responsible for, which filled a whole room and was called a computer. Nobody could have predicted then that fifty years later we'd all be carrying tiny computers around in our pockets and the whole world would be connected via the internet. A world has disappeared in David's lifetime and a new one has come into being. After several jobs in industry and some redundancies he decided to train as a teacher and taught physics for many years in a Technical College. On one occasion, when I was visiting him from Scotland, I went into his classroom to meet him and saw him to be a gentle and dedicated teacher, someone who loved to help young people.

We connected again as I was leaving for New Zealand in the early '90's. He was beginning a new relationship which lasted for nearly twenty years and, although I was happy he had found someone to love, from my perspective as an uncompromising free spirit, I was sorry his preference for the security of a regular working life and a committed relationship didn't leave room for creative self-expression. It was not for me to say that his was not just as valid an approach to life as my own, out there flying solo on a wing and a prayer. In fact, a new partner coming into David's life was a saving grace for both of them, for she too had had a difficult marriage. He was devoted to her for the twenty years they were together, and in the last few years he took care of her when she was immobilized and unwell. The relationship gave David's life meaning and stability and she brought friends and family into his life too. But, like our mother and father before him, I know David never found the creative fulfilment he longed for and I saw the excess weight he carried later in life as an outer manifestation of an inner stagnation. I believe it was this that cost him his health and contributed to his early death at 71.

After his partner's death, David was depressed and isolated and that's when I decided to come back from New Zealand to support him with his dream, which I could see was also the life raft he was clinging to. Outer London where he'd lived for more than thirty years had never felt like home to him and he was ready for his next chapter of life. Now, coming together again in the autumn of our lives, we were two orphans picking over the wreckage of our family life, taking respite in the fragile oasis of companionship we found together.

Making the Break for Freedom

We went on two trips to Wales hunting for land. On the first we explored the border counties between Wales and England and ate a lot of good food in old British inns. On the second trip, in September, we found his plot of land in Pembrokeshire in a small conservation village a few miles from the coast. He fell in love with it at first sight and from that moment it became his obsession. He had to have this bit of land, no other would do. Later, there were some tricky moments when it looked as if the dream might slip through his hands but he was tenacious and clung on.

Once he had found his land it was time to sell his house. This was a huge hurdle for him - to leave his little piece of security and take a leap of faith for himself alone. Yet I could see how much he longed for it. I witnessed his inner conflict, as fear fought with a desire for freedom, and I could empathise as I knew this conflict in myself. One night, around 3am, I was awakened by cries for help and blearily got out of bed to find him sitting on the floor of his bedroom in nothing but his underpants, where he'd fallen and was unable to get up. Fear and helplessness were written all over him. An ungraceful struggle ensued as I tried to work out how to lift him. In his helplessness, he seemed to be playing out his terror of making the move, while at the same time struggling against his dependency. He repeated over and over, "I can't, I can't" and I responded, "Yes, you can. Yes, you can." In the end, I called the ambulance service and two attendants came to hoist him up and reassure him.

After that night, he became more determined. Later, when the house sold, he told me his greatest fear had been that he'd never escape from this cultural desert of London commuter land and he'd be stuck there in this gilded cage for the rest of his life. He'd moved there originally for a job; it was a place in which he'd never really wanted to be and yet he'd stayed for thirty years. He told me many times how excited he was to be moving on and expressed a wistfulness that for all these years he had compromised his "real life" - the life he was meant to have as a creative being.

I watched my brother progress from having a dream, deciding he was going to pursue it, experiencing the deep division created by fear and self-doubt, then moving into a unified certainty and mobilising all his powers to

9

bring the dream into being. Most of us who make our bid for freedom from a life constricted by doubt and the limitations of conditioning, do so much earlier. I made my first break in my twenties, and then again in my early thirties and again around 40. Each time I gained in confidence and trust as I developed skills and understanding to support me for the next leap. By 70, most of us are more fearful and less flexible in every way and it is harder to heave ourselves out of our comfort zones. I appreciated what a huge risk it was for David to break out of his self-imposed prison to pursue his dream. It was a profound irony that a few weeks after he gained his life he also lost it. I'm sure he would still be alive today sitting in front of the TV, with his computer on his lap and the house in chaos, if he hadn't chosen to pursue his dream. But the fact that he took the risk to make this breakthrough makes him my hero. His untimely death, although tragic, occurred at the moment he was experiencing the euphoria of liberation. I believe, summoning the courage to leave his comfort zone and pursue his dream healed his self-esteem and that was a big achievement. What better time to go?

He died suddenly of a massive heart attack three weeks after the move to Pembrokeshire. His mind and spirit were up to the challenge of a new chapter of life but his neglected and ailing body simply couldn't carry on. He was next to the land that was his little bit of Heaven when he passed on, and by all accounts he had become a happy, hopeful and open-hearted man; the man he was always destined to be.

Questions for Inquiry

If you have lost a family member, take some time now to reflect on what you learned about yourself after their death.

Did you make some new choices as a result?

Are there any choices you would like to recommit to now?

Practice: Transforming Reactivity into Acceptance

We all experience reactivity, times when we react to life with stress, impelled by old limiting beliefs and patterns, rather than responding more calmly. We all have old reactive patterns we have been carrying for a lifetime which can be triggered by those we're closest to, particularly family members and partners. The story I've told about how my brother's offers to help me in the kitchen made me feel crowded, is an example. Such occasions are wonderful opportunities to bring awareness into your behaviour and then to make new choices. In this way, as you become more conscious, you can transform lifelong habits of limitation into more loving behaviours.

Develop the Skills of Intention, Awareness, Being Present in the Body and Making Choices

Intention, awareness, presence and choice are the foundational skills of the transformational process.

1. **Start with an intention** to free yourself from limited reactive patterns.

   For example, "I'm ready to free myself now from old reactive patterns that keep me separated from people I love."

   Say your intention out loud and check if it resonates within your body. If not, play with the words until it feels true.

   Write your intention down and put it somewhere you will see it often.

2. The next time you are feeling irritated by a loved one's behaviour, remember your intention and **choose to use it as an opportunity**

to practise. At first you may not be able to do this in the moment, but you can revisit the incident later in your own time.

3. As your irritation arises bring your **awareness** into the sensations in your body and **breathe.** It is very likely your mind will be working overtime, coming up with all sorts of indignant thoughts like, "what do you want from me?", "go away and leave me alone", "get out of my way" "how many times have I told you not to do that!" Do your best not to engage with these thoughts. If you can, just notice them. Are they really a response to what is actually happening now with this person? Is this how you want to be?

4. This mixture of **intention, awareness and becoming present through breathing** should be enough to create a bit of distance between you and your habitual, reactive response.

5. You can then **choose** not to react in your usual irritated way but to simply keep your attention on your breath and stay calm. If the other person enjoys winding you up, saying nothing is a powerful way to interrupt the game.

6. **Try not to judge yourself.** Changing deeply engrained habits is not easy and takes time and repeated practice.

The more frequently you practice the easier it will become. Creating a gap between your conscious, loving, witnessing self and your unconscious habitual reactions frees you to make new choices. Don't get upset if you don't break your reactive pattern the first time, after all this is something you may have been doing for a lifetime and the habit won't be so easily dislodged. Start by stepping away from the situation and working through these steps when you are on your own. Eventually, you will reach a point when you can calm your reactivity in the heat of the moment. Then you can practise telling the other person clearly what you need in the situation, while at the same time acknowledging them. To use the example of my need for space when cooking, eventually I could say something like, "I appreciate your offer of help, maybe you could chop the onions?" Or, "Thanks for offering to help, I'd really like to have a bit of space just now. I'll catch up with you later." Or I might experiment with the new behaviour of enjoying cooking alongside my brother and having fun.

Take your time. The more you do this the more you will come to realise that you really can choose your state of mind and your actions and you don't need to be stuck in old patterns. This is freedom!

Be kind to yourself. Shifting old patterns takes commitment and you may find yourself reacting again and again. Simply re-affirm your intention and keep returning to the practice. The more frequently you practise, the more you will develop new habits which support who you truly are and who you choose to become.

To listen to an audio recording of this practice, including a meditation to help you to become present, go to this webpage: https://www.tribeintransition.net/a-story-of-transformation-free-resources/

The Work of Grief Will Bring You to Your Knees

Over the last twenty-two years I have experienced the deaths of both my parents, my mother in 2001 and my father in 2011; two friends, Joan and Barbara, passed away within a few months of each other in 2004/5 around the age of 50, both with breast cancer; my friend and mentor Bryce died suddenly and unexpectedly in 2011, aged 60 and at the beginning of an exciting, new and much needed chapter of his work in whole person education; Cindy, in Virginia, heroically outlived her doctor's death sentence by two years, a spiritual warrior to the last breath; and then there was Woods.

Was it the accumulation of all this grief that somehow came together after my brother's death and knocked me for six? Loss has a way of gathering to itself all the other losses of a lifetime which have not yet been completed. All my previous grief experiences were partial glimpses into the mystery of life and death, so this present death touched on the one before, and the one before that, and on and on, like a falling pack of cards.

When you know a loved one is departing, as I did with Woods, it can soften the blow considerably. Saying goodbye within a loving relationship can become a time of rich sharing. At the same time, I was deeply moved as I watched him deteriorate and suffer physically. Even if you believe in a soul that journeys on after the body drops away, and you think your friend or family member is going to a haven of love, or setting off on a new adventure, the dying away of the body and personality is still heart rending. In addition to the loss of my friend, Woods' death inevitably raised fears about my own mortality and questions about the nature of death itself.

With David, death came suddenly and unexpectedly. Everything appeared to change in that moment of receiving the bad news. I felt as if a hard spoon cracked down on the eggshell that bound my life together. Like Humpty Dumpty I couldn't imagine how I'd ever be put back together again. I felt out of whack, dazed and confused and I couldn't see any future. My life, which only moments before had a direction and a purpose, now lay in fragments at my feet. I had no idea who I was, why this was happening, or what to do next. There was only this terrible sense of jangling deprivation and startled disbelief. A stinging blow had cruelly shattered my integrity and whatever held my life together was now revealed to be a fragile illusion. Shock affects all dimensions of being and I was quaking in my boots. A coldness crept into my bones and it seemed as if my blood ceased to flow. Shaken to the core, order and stability went flying as I came face to face with death - a non-negotiable reality much more powerful than I will ever be.

This experience of fragmentation manifested in many ways – as emotional numbness, confusion, intense mood swings, physical shakiness, tearfulness, helplessness and raw vulnerability. With my sense of self disrupted and the future eclipsed I was left standing in a precarious, isolated present. No longer able to sense any solid ground beneath me I felt unsupported and diminished.

Shock shook the lid off a Pandora's box of feelings which were too intense to manage all at once: grief, guilt, abandonment, regret, remorse. In addition, present shock can activate old trauma that has not been processed and is held in the body. I couldn't fight this state of overwhelm or bring myself back to "normal" by an act of will. The best I could do was be kind to myself and nurturing. I remembered this too will pass. I took things slow, drank lots of calming tea, wrapped myself in warm blankets and did my best to roll with the punches.

The Funeral and Other Rites of Passage

It was ten days after David's death before the news reached me. Many times I'd cajoled him to make sure he had my name and contact details written down "just in case" but he hadn't done it. Normally we were in touch a few times a week but I hadn't heard from him for a while and I was anxious. In his last message he'd told me he had a tummy bug and was going to the doctor.

The telephone call came at 6pm. His partner's daughter had tracked me down. She told me David had died of a massive heart attack in an apartment right next to his land. She said he'd died immediately and would not have suffered.

Shaking, I put the phone down and called my closest friend, Maggie. As we talked, the most vivid, intense, complete rainbow I have ever seen appeared right in front of my cottage. It was so close and so solid I could almost reach out and touch it. I found it very reassuring as if this was David getting in touch to comfort me. Whenever I see a rainbow now I remember him. The rainbow has become a bridge to my brother and to the afterlife. It's a symbol of joy and connection and represents the hope that we humans can learn to communicate across the differences that seem to divide us from those living in the spirit world, from animals, from all the other kingdoms of nature, from our brothers and sisters whose skin is coloured differently to our own, from those of different cultures, other tongues, diverse ages, and even from our family and loved ones.

The funeral was another bridge and it was my job to arrange it. In a state of shock it's common to lose the focus and energy required for practical tasks and to need help with these undertakings. For me, the practical necessities kept me grounded for short periods each day and helped me to maintain some sense of agency. With my psyche numb and ragged, the acts of finding a funeral director, reaching out to tell friends, choosing music and writing a tribute, helped me to concentrate and find a little relief.

What kind of funeral should I choose? Back in his outer London suburb, David had a scattered network of friends, neighbours, acquaintances, colleagues and students, gathered over the years, but I had no idea how to find them. So I decided to go for a simple cremation service held as near to

David's land as possible. This meant the funeral party was very small and I only had a few people to tell the bad news.

I felt moved to create a funky ceremony that would honour David's soul. I wrote a eulogy, recalling and celebrating his life and spent hours listening to music on YouTube searching for the perfect memories. The song I found that connected me most closely with my brother was, "Little Wing", a Jimi Hendrix song sung by Eric Clapton and Carlos Santana. Music is a direct route to the other's longings and aspirations and these three genius talents of the rock n' roll world summed up who my brother was as I had never heard him express in any other way. I played the song over and over, tears streaming down my face. There was something so sweet and tender, so whimsical and filled with yearning in this song.

> *Well, she's walking through the clouds*
> *With a circus mind that's running wild...*
>
> *When I'm sad she comes to me.*
> *With a thousand smiles she gives to me free.*
> *It's alright, she says, it's alright*
> *Take anything you want from me,*
> *Anything.*
> *Fly on Little Wing*
>
> *– Jimi Hendrix*[1]

https://www.youtube.com/watch?v=PJ-2XFQLZE8

I also found a quotation from Eric Clapton with which I felt sure David would identify:

> *The blues are what I've turned to, what has given me inspiration and relief in all the trials of my life. Music became a healer for me, and I learned to listen with all my being. I found that it could wipe away all the emotions of fear and confusion relating to my family.*[2]

I had done a similar music search for my father's funeral five years earlier, although on that occasion it was operatic arias I was seeking. At this early stage of the death transition, music is the perfect bridge to connect with the essence of the one transitioning to the spirit world and I felt I was making a soul to soul connection with them. At this special time, when the veils between the worlds are thin, I longed to play an active part in supporting my loved ones through their transition. During my grieving for a family member, a close friend or a partner, I have sensed part of me making the journey into the unknown with them. This is impossible to prove and difficult to communicate; but those of you who have experienced something similar will recognise what I am saying. It accounts, in part, for the trouble most of us have in being present to the material world after a significant death when so much of our energy is wrapped up in our own emotions and our soul is reaching into the unknown to be with the other.

When my mother died, I experienced alternate days of numb sorrow and unexpected exaltation. As the grief subsided the experience was overall one of liberation and new beginnings in which I was invited to loaf in a flower-filled meadow, doing nothing and learning how to simply be. A few months later, I had the utterly exhilarating and profoundly scary feeling of standing on the edge of a vast star-filled night sky, a boundless realm of freedom and unending possibility. With my father, I sensed his first few weeks "on the other side" were difficult and full of confusion, and part of me was with him helping him find his way towards the light. With Woods, my attempt to capture the essence of who he was through writing, helped me to stay connected with him.

And now, with David, I was reduced to zero. When I heard the news of his death, it was as if the earth opened beneath my feet and I fell through into a new and unknown place, leaving the self I knew behind, like a sloughed off skin. Perhaps that's how it was for David too in the moment of death. Everything he had been up until then was suddenly whisked away and, with no time to prepare for the journey, he was cast into an unknown realm, in a new beginning he hadn't prepared for.

As I was experiencing these first sharp pangs of loss and the heaviness of bewilderment, organising the funeral helped me to weave joy, connection and celebration into my sorrow. I knew I simply couldn't do it alone and so I asked a friend to drive me down to Pembrokeshire and accompany me, which she kindly agreed to do. Her company made the funeral party into an adventure filled with magical interludes and the promise of good things to come.

The worst moment came when the coffin arrived at the crematorium and I realised with a jolt, yes, my brother's inert, dead body really was here in this box. But where was he? Where was his rock n' roll soul? What happens to all that knowledge, all that life experience? Where does it go? It can't just disappear, can it? Was his spirit here with us, watching?

I certainly felt his presence as I pulled myself together and delivered the eulogy. John McLaughlin and Carlos Santana ushered us into "The House of the Lord"[3] with their plaintive guitars. We whispered our private goodbyes to David and then Eric Clapton sent us on our way, "Over the Rainbow."[4]

As we emerged into the light, summer rain gave way to sunshine and we took off to David's land to toast him with a dram of malt whisky. Being driven along the narrow country roads with their high hedges, I had no idea who I was, where I was, or where I was going, yet I felt totally trusting and light-hearted.

As you journey into a new and unknown world
may you be free from fear and suffering.
May there be friends and helpers
to take your hand when the way is dark,
to comfort you so you never feel scared and alone.
Especially when you feel most lost,
do not despair.

When the light appears
walk towards the Big Light.
Shun the small comforting lights,
walk straight into the light that blazes.

Let go of everything you've clung to,
identification with the body, mind, emotions, stories,
consecrate it all to the fire.
Then may innocence rise:
blank slate, new eyes, open heart.

From "Elegy to My Father", Rose Diamond[5]

I was deeply saddened that David only had three weeks to enjoy his new adventure and so sorry I wouldn't be able to share that adventure with him as I had hoped I would, but I found some consolation in the fact that by embarking on his dream he died happy. From my perspective, he made an astonishing breakthrough, at 71, to leave the home and location in which he had lived for so many years. I honour him for doing that. As we said goodbye to David's body and to his life story, I like to think of his soul travelling on to another adventure, free to start afresh, taking his place in the deep night sky, among the stars.

These two poems speak about the possibilities in death. The first is from Mary Oliver[6] and the second by Kahlil Gibran:[7]

When death comes like an iceberg between the shoulder blades,

I want to step through the door full of curiosity, wondering:
what is it going to be like, that cottage of darkness?

And therefore, I look upon everything as a brotherhood and a sisterhood,

and I look upon time as no more than an idea,

and I consider eternity as another possibility

and I think of each life as a flower

as common as a field daisy, and as singular,

and each name a comfortable music in my mouth.

Kahlil Gibran, On Death

You would know the secret of death.

But how shall you find it unless you seek it in the heart of life?

The owl whose night-bound eyes are blind unto the day cannot

unveil the mystery of light.

If you would indeed behold the spirit of death, open your heart

wide unto the body of life.

For life and death are one, even as the river and the sea are one.

In the depth of your hopes and desires lies your silent knowledge

of the beyond;

And like seeds dreaming beneath the snow your heart dreams of

spring.

Trust the dreams, for in them is hidden the gate to eternity.

Questions for Inquiry

These questions will bring rewards whether the person you choose to contemplate has died or has moved on into a new stage of life without you.

1. Take some time to sit with your memories of your loved one and simply be with whatever arises in your thoughts and feelings.

   If you have a photo of them, or a piece of music they loved, this can be a powerful way of connecting. If tears come, let them flow. Make space for all your emotions and simply notice and honour them.

   What do you most love and appreciate about this beloved person?

What, if anything, feels unfinished in this relationship?

How might you find completion now?

2. When you are ready, write about your loved one or draw them.

    Speak to them and imagine what they, in turn, want to say to you.

3. When you have finished go outside into nature and breathe.

    Feel your feet on the ground and the air on your skin.

    Empty your mind.

What is Grief and Why is it Important?

The Labour of Grieving

> *Most important of all, death is an invitation to become aware of whatever has been limiting our expression of love so that we may choose to love and live fully. Isn't that what we're here for?*

The real work of grieving started after the funeral. David had gone and now the journey of moving towards acceptance began. My brother's death reminded me that grief is a mysterious and complex process which unfolds in its own time. While some talk about stages of grief, I see it as a natural process that has its own rhythm and flows at its own pace, as long as we don't disrupt it. It's something we must experience, attend to, and learn to move with. Grief can be emotionally overwhelming at times, but within it we have choices. We can choose to fully feel our grief, give it the space it needs, and allow it to guide us through to new life.

Grieving is a unique journey for everyone and no two grieving journeys are ever the same. Each time we are beginners entering new territory. Because grief is part of being human there are common themes and feelings but, although we may empathise, we can never fully understand another's grief. This tends to make grieving a lonely time. Introspection and intense emotions aren't much encouraged in our society and so we may fear that if we travel inwards we will wander too far from the crowd and get lost in sadness. We may judge ourselves for how we grieve, put a lid on our feelings or try to rush through it. But I want to encourage you to fly in the face of social expectations and stay with your grief until you are complete with it. It will strengthen and deepen you and make you wiser.

As I was grieving for my brother, my initial experience of shock and raw vulnerability, the feelings of being ungrounded and not quite of this world, passed. And then, after the funeral, I settled into what I call the labour of grieving. I use labour here both to name the work that is involved and to point to grieving as a movement through death to new life, a birthing process. This lasted initially for a few months and by November I was feeling more buoyant. In December, I took off back to New Zealand for a four-month visit, during which time I felt light, joyful and free. I thought my grieving was complete but when I returned to Wales after the visit I entered a second phase of deeper grief which lasted over several years. Don't let that alarm you because this story too has brought many valuable gifts and I will share these with you soon. But now, I'd like to weave together the threads of my grieving as I experienced them during these first few months after David's death; threads which together wove a container for the transformation to come.

Feel Your Loss Fully

One thread of grief is the personal loss we feel. In the first few months following David's death, I was fully submerged in this experience of loss.

I missed my brother every day, many times a day, all day, in the background of my mind and amidst any activity, David was calling my name. I missed the regular contact we'd had; I was bound up in his story, woven into it, a leading player. Even when living at a distance we'd been in contact several times a week. But the loss went deeper than that. David was the last remaining person on Earth who had known me all my life. We carried a shared history, albeit our accounts of that history were from our own individual points of view. We hadn't always been close, but, despite the physical distance and the years between our meetings, we had been friends and allies.

In our months of living together, we were beginning to explore and grow our brother and sister friendship and I had been looking forward to more. I didn't realise until he'd gone how much I was counting on it. He had become a rock in my landscape: a safe, stable presence who would always be a shelter in a storm for me; a form of security I could hold onto to make me feel safe and less alone. I was sad for us both that the story of his eco-home in Pembrokeshire had come to such an abrupt and sorry end. I'd thought I had plenty of time to visit him there and harboured "odd couple" dreams of building a cabin in the corner of his garden and mellowing into old age together, still rocking with Santana and Eric Clapton, until the distant day we died. When my brother left his body, he took with him this future I had been dreaming into being. The dream evaporated into an empty thought form, an illusion of certainty, where in fact there was no certainty at all.

Celebrate and Touch Souls

Losing someone close to you is never easy. But throughout my grieving process for David, I found little moments of joy that helped balance out the sadness. Planning his funeral and writing the tribute gave me a chance to focus on the memories we shared. There were many rainbows which drew surges of joy from me when they appeared. I tuned in to the radio every Saturday to two jazz shows he loved, to feel connected with him. I inherited his car and listened to his music when I was driving. Simple things like using some of his pots and pans brought back fond memories of the meals we had together and I felt David right there with me.

I discovered death doesn't have to end a relationship after the loved one has gone. It can actually provide an opportunity to get to know the other person better. When David was alive, I'm sad to say I rarely thought of spending time with him. But after his death he had my whole attention and I made the space to enter into his story with my imagination. I could be curious and feel into who he really was in a way that perhaps was not possible when he was alive. The same was true for my mum and dad. Going back through photos and memories with an open mind, I felt I was getting to know them on a deeper level. I felt their essences and touched souls with them. It was comforting to feel David's spirit and remember our bond didn't end just because his physical body was gone. We remain connected to those we love, even after death. Their essence lives on through the impact they had on our lives and the memories we cherish. Making space for the grieving process and taking all the time I needed helped me to feel less alone and to find meaning during a difficult time.

Experience Empathy

*The work of grief is in allowing our humanity, in all its
aspects, to move through us and to transform the heart.*

As I delved deeper into my brother's story, I also mourned his unrealized
potential, his sorrows, and all the ways his life was limited by circumstances
beyond his control which then affected his personality. David's passing
came so soon after he had finally started living the life he truly wanted and,
in my early grief, I felt this was unfair and tragic, the ultimate injustice.
Over the following months, I reflected on how he had struggled against the
difficult hand he was dealt: an abusive father who rejected him; a profoundly
disabled son; a messy divorce; many job losses and moves to places he
otherwise wouldn't have chosen; a lonely search for love and fulfilment.

My brother's missed chances and heartaches mirrored back to me
my own sorrows, dreams not achieved, failures and unwise choices. This
suffering felt intensely personal and yet also universal. By allowing myself to
grieve, I remembered hardship is part of the shared human experience and
none of what we endure is entirely personal. We all mess up, we all fail, we
all fall short of who we could be. A mix of empathy and imagination helped
me to shift my attention beyond my own story and into the bigger story of
humanity. We are all so attached to our individuality and yet, whenever I
take the time and care to reflect on my own or another's life, I see how each
of us is an opening into a shared narrative.

As I contemplated my brother's life I sometimes saw him as one tiny fractal of the whole of a humanity that has been oppressed and repressed through the ages. Feeling keenly into this travesty of human nature, and how our collective well-being, our creativity and our capacity to participate fully in a common story have been affected, enabled me to deepen my compassion for all beings. This was a profound expansion of love and meaning.

The work of grief is in allowing our humanity, in all its aspects, to move through us and to transform the heart. Feeling into my brother's losses brought me closer to him. I felt I was mourning *with* him and I imagined him burning off his old story and attachments as he passed into the next dimension of the spirit world lighter and freer.

Forgive Yourself and Make New Choices

As grief opened my heart, and David's physical presence was no longer here, it was easy to forget all the little ways I'd felt separate from him; how he'd driven me to hair-pulling exasperation or failed to live up to what I wanted him to be. As I began to see him more clearly, I needed to forgive myself. I hadn't had a chance to say goodbye, to tell him I loved him, to say sorry for my impatience, irritability and judgments, to make amends for not being there more fully, for not being nearly as skilled as I needed to be. My shortcomings showed me how I could be more openly loving in future but with David it was too late. Especially with family, the desire to forgive, love and communicate is matched by the powerful, deeply entrenched entropy of family habits and resentments. Sadly, it often takes death or the loss of a relationship to tear through these veils of inertia. Death is the vacuum cleaner coming for all those strong and sticky cobwebs. It's the Great Awakener.

It was tempting to see my brother's death from the spiritual perspective that each of us is given exactly what we need for our growth and to view the timing of his death as a completion of what he had come to learn this time around. This may be true and yet it is so important to allow space for the very human feelings of remorse, anger at injustice and deep sadness, as they arise, rather than rationalising them away. A little remorse is a good thing – it points to where we can make new choices and attempt to be better people. But we need to avoid drowning in guilt and getting stuck in "if only..." What has happened has happened and the only thing we have control over is how we behave from this moment on. So I sat with my self-reproach until it faded but the pain of knowing I could have loved more and better is still with me as a constant reminder to be kind.

Cleaning Cupboards

In those first few months I spent many hours every day collapsed on the sofa watching television while the threads of my inner world unfolded through and around me. Gradually my reveries became interwoven with plans and dreams for the future, as life reached towards me and drew me out. But before I could move forward into a new chapter I had my brother's worldly possessions to sort and dispose of. I felt lucky everything was gathered together in storage rather than having a house to empty. However, when I visited the warehouse to find out what was there, and the doors were rolled back, I groaned with dismay to discover four storage rooms all packed to the ceiling, three of them a jumbled chaos. Apparently, David hadn't sorted anything before the move but had thrown it all in higgledy-piggledy for some future day.

I was determined to get the job done as fast as possible, not least because the fees were excessive, but also because to empty these rooms would mark a form of closure and open the way forward. My coming trip to New Zealand during the UK winter provided a motivational timeline. I set out blithely with the intention to get the closet cleaning done within one week and invited two of David's friends to help me for a couple of days, which they kindly agreed to do.

I'm sure you will have experienced your own times of sorting and emptying cupboards. We humans are such acquisitive beings it's an ongoing task for most of us to keep emptying out all the things we thought we couldn't live without. Unfortunately, this wasn't a task my brother had applied himself to with any enthusiasm and, in addition to his own lifetime of hoarding, he had also taken in piles of stuff from our parents' home after Dad's death.

On one level those days in the warehouse were plain hard work. On another level, it was a form of soul weaving. Not only was I witnessing my brother's life, as it emerged from the boxes of papers, clothes and sundry artefacts, but I was also able to piece together more of the family story.

A paper trail mapped David's career, going back to the 1970's, with payslips, CVs, job applications, rejection and acceptance letters. These early papers were easily disposed of, and, in those first two days, with three of us working together, we moved a few hundredweight of paper and assorted bric-a-brac to the recycling centre. But, after David's friends had returned home, it became a slower business as the more recent papers had to be looked at and considered. I sat on a little stool, on the cold concrete floor, in the gloomy warehouse, with the autumn sun shining enticingly outside, for six hours every day. Then, I staggered wearily back to my rented apartment, overlooking David's land, stiff with mental and emotional fatigue, to collapse once more in front of the TV, with a comforting cup of tea.

I was on an emotional roller coaster and, because I needed to keep moving, I let it all flow through me. Moments of frustration: "how could you keep all these shopping bills and used up lottery tickets!" were followed by heart moving tenderness as I read through the correspondence between David and his ex-wife or came across a few scribbled words describing his heartache when searching for love. I saw how emotionally damaging and financially stressful the experience of divorce had been for him. Like most of us he wanted to love and be loved and to be happy, and yet, when love has been absent or inconsistent in childhood and you start off with a low tank of self-esteem, every failure of love, and every rejection, takes its toll.

And then there were the unlived dreams – five guitars nestled in their cases: two acoustic, two electric rhythm and one bass – all barely played, and carefully locked away, cherished and saved for the quiet days at the end of the rainbow, which never came. There were three cameras but not an interesting photo in sight. There was the first page of a book he had imagined writing about quantum physics and the universe. Our father had accused David, from an early age, of being "lazy" and said he "didn't apply himself" and I wondered now about these unlived dreams and creative aspirations. How is it some of us pursue the creative muse no matter what, whilst others don't make it past the starting line? Was he unmotivated? Too lacking in confidence? Was it as much as he could manage to keep the money coming in and, in his later years, take care of a disabled partner? Clearly, having a creative life was not his priority. Yet, these unlived dreams, this broken heart, alongside the happy holiday snaps, the blue suede shoes, his love of physics and music, touched my heart and teased me into thought.

Here was a human life packed into cardboard boxes in these dusty rooms; a human identity, a story no longer required. All the shirts, the jackets and books, the dinner services, fine glasses and broken coffee pots, had to go somewhere. Who wanted them? Where would they all end up? We're a species of collectors, like magpies attracted to shiny new things, we like to take more than we need. If we see it we want it and when we want it we have to have it. I had visions of humanity drowning under the detritus of our desire for more and more things to fill up our inner craving.

David's friends urged me to get rid of it all and make a new start. I reluctantly gave away the good furniture to charity and found a dry stone shed on the land where everything I wanted to keep fitted nicely into the available space. I stored the guitars, all the music – David's jazz and rock, my dad's opera and classical - a few books and some fine china; a huge pile of gardening magazines. I left the laughing Buddha sitting under the mature ash tree in the corner of the garden and planted primroses around him.

It took thirteen days to complete the clearance, a feat of determination and perseverance. I was relieved when it was done.

You Don't Have to Grieve Alone

Grief can be the loneliest of life's events. I have found that during the intense rawness of grief, even though I might feel desperately lonely and greatly in need of another's care, I usually don't want to talk to anyone. In my sensitive and under-resourced state contact with others feels too risky. I don't have the words and I don't trust people to respond in a way that I will feel met. I've talked with friends about this and many of them agreed that, in the acute phase of grief, even the closest loved ones – partners, family members and dear friends – can be a cause of irritation and alienation. At those times when we are feeling most vulnerable, tender and unguarded and we crave care, any false note or failure to connect with another can feel demoralising. Even though I am an advocate for coming together in groups to share our experiences, there is a time for solitary contemplation and mobilising our own strength and courage.

But there is also a time when it is healthy to come out of isolation and my writing provided a lifeline for reaching out to friends. I wrote the first draft of this book in those first few months of grief and when it was finished I was eager share it. On my return to New Zealand, I gave copies of the book to friends who were all healing practitioners and I invited them into conversations with me to explore our experiences of grief and loss. When we came together to sit in circle, each woman spoke in response to whatever memories and experiences my writing had touched in her. Although we were all familiar with sitting in circles and exploring deeply, we were nervous at first. Every person in that group had grieved deeply at one time or another but this was the first time we had ventured into the territory of grief so explicitly together. Yet, by the end of our first round of sharing, the atmosphere in the room had transformed. Nervousness and tension were replaced with lightness and an almost tangible feeling of love, even grace, prevailed. Creating this time and space and giving each other encouragement to speak of our grief, and from our grief, brought relief. This simple act of participation connected us, one to another, at the heart.

That first meeting with a circle of friends sowed the seeds for what later became *The Sitting with Death and Choosing Life Programme*,[8] I didn't set out to create a programme but this body of work revealed itself and grew bit by bit over the next few years, as I followed my curiosity. I was so inspired by this first group conversation I followed by recording conversations with some of the individuals in the group, inviting each person to share her story and wisdom. These were the first *Sitting with Death and Choosing Life Conversations*[9], which grew into a library of over fifty recorded dialogues. These are now used as stimulus materials for conversation circles. In my experience, grief and creativity are interwoven. While grief deepens our understanding of what it means to be human, creativity can lift the heavy weight of grief and transform it into gifts that can be shared.

31

Renewal

My trip to New Zealand, six months after David's death, was the completion of this first phase of grief. Here's what I wrote about it:

"Now a weight has lifted from me, I am feeling profound gratitude. Little by little, bit by bit, I am beginning to live in the present moment, free to just be. The grief work continues more gently now. With each choice I consider what I truly want, wary of falling back on old habitual likes and dislikes or becoming caught up in addictive longing. I am tasting everything, as if for the first time, and then deciding if I want to say yes or no based on whether it will increase my well-being or detract from it. This brings me into the presence of beginner's mind and to the well-spring of creative play.

I'm living freely in the moment and, at the same time, I have a sense of having arrived somewhere, on the other side of a transition, perhaps? I am writing these pages back in the little paradise of Golden Bay, New Zealand, where I lived for many years. A sweet breeze is rustling the trees and swallows have come to perch on the wires of a kiwifruit vine just two metres in front of my chair. I'm reclining here, perfectly relaxed, gazing admiringly at the velvety blooms of potted flowers with their deep crimson, scarlet, mauve, pink and pale green crowns. I love the way they turn their faces to the sky and drink in the liquid sun, celebrating their own vibrancy and beauty while providing a feast for my eyes. This is a world in which every being, every creature, is encouraged to flower. It's a far cry from the world at large with its extreme chaos and disarray. The world as we have known it is disappearing fast and we stand at the brink of a collective death. All around the planet many of us are grieving for our world and we don't know if we will survive the mayhem to come."

In this relaxed, open state, I received the following message from Woods:

I'm here in bliss and ecstasy, Rosy, and when you are in joy I can reach you. You know joy is what I was always longing for. But in life I was constantly chasing it and the chasing held me back. When you chase anything, it does the natural thing – it runs away. It's important to learn to sit and wait, empty of expectation and need.

I liked being high. I was addicted to spiritual highs as much as any other sort but you can't just turn the other way and try to avoid the pain of being human. If pain doesn't have a place to be expressed it eats away at you or constricts you until you can barely breathe, and then snuffs you out.

I was ready to be rid of the body, Rosy. You know how much I suffered physically for the last twenty years of my life. And I did that very male thing, I put a brave face on it, I kept myself to myself, I feasted alone at the table of discontent. My body became increasingly weak and twisted out of shape. Bits fell off, other bits failed to play their part. It was a steady and unrelenting one-way ticket to deconstruction. And while my mind was struggling to accept the limitations that grew and multiplied within my physical vehicle, my spirit was becoming all the more desperate for space in which to unfold my eagle wings and fly, held by the slip stream, without a doubt or a care, not a rule in sight. Free to go beyond all imaginary limits and further still beyond the power of the imagination.

I held this tension in myself all those years – on the one hand the failing body, and on the other the aspiring free spirit. The conclusion was inevitable. I had to cast my skin and go find out how it is to be skinless for a while.

Rosy, in those suffering years you helped to ease my pain and I am eternally thankful. Your enthusiasm was balm for my soul, a goddess breath of fresh air straight off the mountains. Your seemingly never-ending crystal stream of divine inspiration and evolutionary fervour cascaded upon my dusty dry lips and woke me up.

And now I finally see you in your wholeness and your radiance, sitting in a meadow of buttercups, red and white clover, long grasses nodding sagely in the breeze. The mountains are before you and there's blue sky, deep heavenly blue, with puffy dancing white clouds and the sun beaming on you. And closer in there's a line of eucalyptus standing tall, rustling their silver leaves. And, as the sunbeams dance on the leaves, the trees are on fire with enthusiasm, just as sunlight dances on water, until you don't know what is water and what is light; what is light and what is tree? What is you and what is me?

You gaze at the clouds and try to decipher the messages in their shapeshifting. You think I'm out there somewhere and I am … but I'm also right here with you.

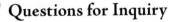

Questions for Inquiry

What have been some of the most challenging aspects of grieving for you?

What helped you through the hard times?

And what were the gifts?

Practice: Allowing All Your Feelings

Being present with all your feelings as they arise is another simple, but not easy, practice that can help to transform your life. Once again, the more frequently you practise the more quickly you will notice the results. I suggest you start with just five minutes once a day, sitting with your eyes closed. And then, when you are feeling more confident with it you can take five minutes several times a day with open eyes, walking or going about your daily life. This practice is a tool that will help you to switch on the light of awareness at any time.

For the first week, take five minutes every morning to sit in a comfortable place where you won't be disturbed.

Close your eyes and begin by breathing gently through your body, simply following your breath with your awareness. Don't try to change anything just notice what's here.

You may notice resistance arising as a tightening in your belly or in your hands. You may feel irritated, restless or distracted. Just notice and bring your attention to the energy in your body.

Or you may notice sadness as a heaviness in your chest or a tingling around your eyes. Again, just notice and bring your attention to the energy in your body.

On the other hand, you may be feeling excited, impatient and eager to move.

Whatever is here, give it your attention. If there are thoughts, do your best to ignore them. If there are judgments, let them go. If the whole five minutes goes by and you haven't noticed a thing, don't worry. Renew your intention and come back tomorrow.

Over time, this practice will free your emotional energy and allow it to move through you. You will become more aware of all the ways you judge yourself and you will be free to make different choices. As your emotional energy flows more freely, you will feel more alive and more able to participate in life creatively.

Don't forget to listen to the audio recording of this practice, which includes a meditation, here: https://www.tribeintransition.net/a-story-of-transformation-free-resources/

This poem by Rumi beautifully describes this art of allowing. [10]

The Guest House

This being human is a guest house.
Every morning a new arrival…

The dark thought, the shame, the malice.
meet them at the door laughing and invite them in.

Be grateful for whatever comes.
because each has been sent
as a guide from beyond.

The Gifts of Grieving

Of all the gifts my brother's death delivered to me, the wake-up
call to love more generously is the most precious.

Grieving Well Means Completing One of Life's Most Difficult Tasks

The death of a loved one has always been a special time for me, despite my sadness at the loss. Coming face to face with death can wake me out of my comfort zone, cut through everyday habit, remind me of the bigger context in which we live and help me to embrace both my human and my spiritual nature. It opens a door to the mystery of what happens to us after we die, and what, if anything, comes next. Death reminds me I am a soul here on Earth to experience everything, to realize my full human potential and to participate in the conscious evolution of my species.

Death is fundamental to the human experience, its inevitability gives a finite timeframe and draws a boundary around a life – I don't know when I am going to die but I do know it will happen. Most of the time I can go along quite happily forgetting this fact, I'm far too busy thinking about what I have to do today to worry about dying. Then suddenly a loved one passes on, a friend receives a sobering health diagnosis, there is a global catastrophe or a terrorist attack, and then I am jolted out of my comfort zone and I remember, oh yes, life is precious, life is a gift. Am I making the best use of the gifts I've been given?

If you have recently lost a loved one – a sibling, a parent, a partner or beloved friend, then you may agree with me that grieving can be a sacred practice. Grief lifts us out of everyday habit-bound experience and clears a space for reflecting on life and death. It's a time to honour and celebrate the life of the one who has passed on; a time to feel your love for them and to renew your healthy self-love. We may also come to see ourselves and our behaviour and how we affect others more clearly. As we let go of whatever is no longer loving and life-giving, acceptance and forgiveness arise and we are able to make new, more life-affirming, choices and to practice more compassionate behaviours.

You may also agree with me that grief is challenging. As death shakes us awake it shows us everything in ourselves that is preventing us living fully - the little grudges we carry, the slights of others that have upset us and the wounds we are nursing. We can see what is important to us and what no longer serves our wellbeing. Death illuminates the underground web of self-doubt that sprouts up like weeds after a shower of rain and shows us what is asking to be released and healed. All of this may initially bring a deeper sense of loss. It can be quite shocking when the veils are swept away and unloving or dysfunctional aspects of your behaviour are revealed. And yet, these uncomfortable revelations are ultimately liberating. I still cringe today at the ways I judged my brother, distanced myself from him and was stingy with my love and attention. And yet I can see how my remorse has changed me for the better. Of all the gifts my brother's death delivered to me, this wake-up call to love more generously is the most precious.

If you are in a grieving process now, or coming to the end of a period of grief, and you have taken time out from your everyday concerns to give grief the attention it calls for; if you have allowed yourself to feel, at least some of the time, the raw emotions of loss, including feelings of abandonment, anger, confusion, sorrow and despair; if mourning for your loved one has shown you any little ways you might love more fully or say yes to life more wholeheartedly; then, you have completed one of life's most difficult tasks. I honour you for that.

Through Grief We Can Deepen Our Understanding of What it Means to be Human

When a person you love dies, they leave a hole in your life that can never be filled by someone or something else. The person you love has gone and, if it was a loving relationship, you miss him or her, sometimes more than you can bear. If it wasn't a loving relationship or there was a lot of conflict, there's grieving to do for the relationship you didn't have. In either case, there will be healing and forgiveness and compassion to find, a closure of some kind. Sometimes closure can take years. You may try to fill the hole created by death with another person, or with whatever eases your distress. But no one else can ever fill the space in my heart that has my brother's name on it, or the hole that Woods left. Grieving is a willingness to enter that hole, to fully experience the loss and the emptiness and the raw pain, as an honouring of the one who has gone, your relationship with them and our common humanity.

Grief is a natural process shared by all humans and other animals, we experience sadness and loss when someone who has been important to us leaves us. In an ideal scenario a person would live to a ripe old age and die fulfilled after putting their affairs in order and saying goodbye to loved ones. In such a case, for those left behind, grieving may be a gentle process of remembering and celebrating the life of the one departing. My experience with Woods came close to this as he had attempted to live a conscious life and die a conscious death but, even so, the months after his death were marked by gravitas. I went away on a solitary retreat for three months so that I could have that special time, in the space between worlds, with him. There was nothing else more important. Even though I had said goodbye to him while he was alive, I needed to say a deeper goodbye, a goodbye in which I could integrate the fruits of our relationship into my being. And that takes time and attention.

Most deaths do not comply with any ideal scenario. Most deaths, like most human relationships, are messy. But we always have the choice to grieve consciously. Loss and grief are natural parts of the cycle of life and death in which every living being is born, matures and passes away and yet grieving is something most of us in the West must learn how to do well. The western culture does not encourage sadness or emotional release and has no rituals, apart from the funeral, to mark this loss. Instead, we are mostly taught to stuff down our feelings and bury them under mounds of food, alcohol, cigarette fumes, drugs, adrenaline rushes, compulsive exercise, addictive sex, tv, social media, shopping and overwork. The sad and disturbing feelings don't go away, they get buried in the body and in the mind, where they drain us of energy and weigh us down.

When I was working as a psychotherapist, I listened to the stories of people who had lost a parent as a child and had not been given space or encouragement to grieve. This is a sure recipe for confusion and fear that can last into adulthood and shape the life story of the individual. When we have been taught to hold back tears, to maintain some notion of professionalism at work or to preserve an image of being the strong one who can hold it all together for the sake of the family, the energy required to repress intense emotion contributes to the high incidence of heart disease, as well as other fatal diseases, as the unprocessed emotions sit heavy on the heart and squeeze the other organs.

Choosing to grieve consciously means taking the space and making the time to be with your memories and all the feelings that arise in you. It means becoming curious about the person who has passed on, who were they really? What challenges were they facing? How did their being in this world make a difference to you? Who were you in relation to them? Did you make the most of the relationship, or not? Are there any ways you will choose to be different going forward?

Through grieving we have the opportunity to find the gifts in adversity and come to a place of acceptance with what is and with what has been, so we may move forward strengthened, regenerated, and with a deeper understanding of what it means to be human. As we come to accept our shortcomings and those of our loved ones, and we own our strengths, we develop a wiser and kinder attitude to humanity and to life at large.

I have no doubt I am a more loving person now as a result of the time I had with my brother before he died and the grieving I have done since. The shock of his death revealed to me all the little ways I separated myself from him and all the ways I judged him, and this has enabled me to make new, kinder choices. I would go as far as to say that letting my brother into my heart has allowed me to fully join the human family, whereas before I tried to hold myself separate. I have a much deeper and more compassionate understanding of the human condition now I have dismounted from my high horse and hung up the armour of the solitary, spiritual warrior.

Death Invites Us to Develop a Greater Capacity to Love and Live Fully

As result of the insights I gathered through reflecting on the early family life I shared with my brother, I am finally learning to draw clear boundaries which also allow people to come in closer. Four years ago I began a new relationship with a man with whom I now live. This has been an ongoing education in maintaining my autonomy while being close.

Most important of all, death is an invitation to become aware of whatever has been limiting our expression of love so that **we may choose to love and live fully.** For me, this is no longer a longing for the fulfilment of romantic love or grand adventures. Loving and living are expressed through a series of small, daily choices.

> *Freedom. It isn't once, to walk out*
> *Under the Milky Way, feeling the rivers*
> *of light, the fields of dark –*
> *freedom is daily, prose-bound, routine*
> *remembering. Putting together, inch by inch*
> *the starry worlds. From all the lost collections.*
>
> Adrienne Rich, For Memory[11]

Death Calls us to a Deeper Purpose

Contemplating my brother's life taught me how much the trauma of domestic abuse can have lifelong effects on our happiness and rob us of the ability to make space for creative self-expression. My brother's struggle to liberate himself cost him his life and revealed to me the heroic journey we humans make in order to be autonomous, self-actualising, creative beings living our own destiny. He reminded me just how important our choices for creative self-expression are.

When grief and loss are not addressed and given space this results in a stagnation of energy within the body and a numbing of the mind, which robs us of vitality, intelligence and freedom. I came to see how we are living within a global pandemic of unprocessed grief and this fired me with a mission to raise awareness of grief and pass on the skills and understandings I have learned to others – to educate, encourage, empower and equip people to meet the challenges of the grieving process. This renewed sense of meaning, purpose and direction has given me endless opportunities for creative work, self-expression and connecting with others in meaningful ways.

Finding those things that fire your heart and your imagination, and following your passion, will keep you alive.

We Can Renew Ourselves

Maybe it was because David's death was sudden or because he was my final relative, leaving me the last one standing; or perhaps the timing for the transformation grief offers was written in my soul's DNA. Whatever the reason, David's death, following so soon on the loss of Woods, was a catalyst for a major process of letting go and renewal within me which has unfolded over several years. Not every grieving process results in such a transformation and although this was one of the most challenging times of my life, I feel privileged to have experienced this. It has strengthened and softened me, made me more resilient and flexible.

The unravelling of the old identity, which facing into death may set in motion, can be very challenging. Nevertheless whenever this opportunity arises, seize it.

For David
He aint heavy, he's my brother

The road is long
With many a winding turn
That leads who knows where
Who knows where …?
But I'm strong, strong enough to carry him.
He aint heavy, he's my brother…
He aint heavy, he's my brother.

The Hollies[12]

https://www.youtube.com/watch?v=eUWZqbumaZo

Chapter Two

Conscious Healing

Urgent as our existential crisis is, the evolution of consciousness can't be hurried, it unfolds in its own time. But we can learn to co-operate with it. Grieving, healing, creating and transforming are pathways through which we can learn the skills of co-operation.

The first part of my story has been about personal grief, now we're going to turn our attention to transpersonal grief and how our individual efforts at healing can benefit the collective and contribute to the process of conscious evolution.

Sometimes death and grief visit briefly. We shed tears, we miss the other, we feel the pain of loss; the veil between everyday reality and the deeper mysteries of life and death is drawn back for a while. And then, events close around us again, we must return to work, pay the bills and feed the family, there is no time to loiter in this in-between realm.

There are also times for a deeper relationship with grief. If death is a call to open our hearts, to love more fully and to live more wholeheartedly, the conscious healing process invites us deeper into a dedicated process of deep introspection through which we can find the courage to let go of whatever is limiting us. The sifting and sorting of memory and experience is the labour of the conscious healing process and is potentially transformative and redemptive. Some of us are naturally drawn to being conscious healers just as others are born to be scientists or gardeners; it is our soul work – what we came here to do. As our collective existential crises deepen many more of us are being called to this mission. As a species, we urgently need to shift into a unified consciousness which honours both life and death – only this will enable us to survive and create a future worth living. This requires us to empty out all the old conditioning that limits us – the limiting beliefs of an old materialistic paradigm that no longer supports life. The remainder of this book is dedicated to an exploration of what this means and how we may do this.

Grieving for a Family Member Can Ripple Out into the Healing of Humanity

I believe we are being called to a collective rite of passage by our species' Soul, the dimension of consciousness that holds the deepest wisdom, meaning, purpose and direction for our collective journey of evolution. It holds the biggest purpose or grand design for the project of humanity – our most profound meaning for being here on Earth at this time - which is to bring together into one, whole, integrated, embodied being, our human and our spiritual natures.

While I was visiting in New Zealand it seemed my labour of grief was over and I was free to begin a new chapter of life. However, when I returned to my cottage in Wales, in April 2017, I sat on the sofa all day long that first day, shivering and paralysed by the cold damp spring air. I felt like a bird that had been flying through the freedom of a big blue sky and then I had fallen suddenly to earth like a stone, into a small cold puddle.

Now a deeper healing began as I revisited the shock of my brother's death all over again. I felt utterly alone with no family and, because I had only recently come to live in this part of the world, I had no friends or community locally either. Before my trip overseas my time had been filled with organising the funeral, grieving, writing and then getting ready to travel. Now there was nothing to fill the space. It never occurred to me to jump on another plane and fly back to New Zealand, I felt there was a reason for me to be here in the UK, but I had no idea yet what it was. Normally, I love solitude and can keep myself amused for weeks on end but now I was dismayed to re-enter grief and even more dismayed when this turned out to be the prolonged process I came to call "my seven years of grief".

I've had a keen interest in the process of psycho-spiritual transformation and the creative process of conscious evolution for many years, but it was only now at the age of 67, that grief moved in, took up its abode within me and demanded that I enter into a conscious relationship with it. This reflected my own readiness and, as the only surviving family member, it was a special opportunity to see more clearly into family dynamics and to heal these within myself. Although I began writing this book as a way to support myself through grief and to better understand the grieving process, very soon it grew into an inquiry that moved me beyond my individual concerns. First, I came to understand how the death of a family member can be a catalyst for healing the family and how this can then ripple out into the healing of humanity. Then, with COVID and lockdown in 2020, my grief expanded again into heartbreak for our world. With a deepening awareness of how life itself is threatened by unconscious human actions, I realised how the skills of sitting with death, grieving well and emerging from grief to choose life, are vital to our individual and collective wellbeing.

Woven into my sorrow for our world was a fresh realisation of the extraordinary heroic journey we humans are on to free ourselves from the limitations of the conditioned mind and how an inner psycho-spiritual dying and rebirth is essential to this heroic journey. I had experienced in an earlier life transition the stark feeling of emptiness I was feeling now as I sat on my sofa in shock on that April day. I sensed I was being called to my next stage of this transformational journey, to my own inner dying, and I didn't feel ready. I feared the falling away of my old self, even though I knew I had outgrown it, and I dreaded the lonely descent into renewal. I would have loved to find a way to avoid what I knew was coming but already I felt helpless in the face of the inevitable.

I know I am not alone in experiencing the deep descent into healing I am about to recount. Many of the people I work with are conscious healers and have been on a spiritual path for many years, so they are not new to the labour of grief, but there has definitely been a new intensity in the collective healing process over these last few years. Many have been moving through difficult inner transitions, whether these were sparked by the death of a loved one, the pain of a friend's suicide, the ending of a life chapter, health

45

challenges, or the loss of hope in the face of the climate emergency and the extinction of species. The multiple, interwoven, life-threatening crises across our world are perilous in the extreme and yet running through them there is an evolutionary impulse which offers us the choice to heal ourselves at the deepest possible level, to open our hearts and to become a movement for compassion and unity around the planet.

The Soul's mission is to build a bridge between our individual stories, our common humanity, and our place in the grander web of life, so that we can bring these three threads of our being and consciousness into creative harmony.

Each of us comes into life with a particular path to follow and a role for which we are ideally suited. Some of us are called to teaching, others to science, to be an artist, an engineer or a gardener, for instance. Some are called to be conscious healers. Conscious healing is the transformational process through which we release whatever is preventing us from experiencing our essential wholeness so that we can become more loving, more compassionate, more peaceful and live with gratitude and generosity, in harmony with life. Difficult life experiences can be used to deepen and expand our knowing of what it means to be human. At the same time our spiritual understandings and practices open us to a more integrated consciousness which includes both our human and our spiritual experience. This process of transformation typically requires us to let our old, limited identities fall away so that a new, more expanded consciousness can emerge. This integrated consciousness then ripples out to others as we connect and, by its very nature, it can touch and change people.

Integrated consciousness is the essential building block for creating the new, life-affirming culture that we need in order for life on Earth to flourish.

Learning to Grieve Well is Essential to
the Conscious Healing Process

*It is only by facing into death that we can come to a full understanding of what
it means to be human. And it is only by fully embracing our human-ness that
we can step into our destiny as spiritual beings having a human experience.*

I developed my understanding of the conscious healing process by living
it, and by reflecting on my brother's life and on my own. As I did so, I
realized just how much death and grief have been exiled to the shadows of
our culture and to the edges of our psyches, and the extent of the negative
impact of this on our individual and collective well-being. We know death
and grief are here with us somewhere but they have been locked away behind
the door of taboo and we have had little or no relationship with them. We
have been taught to fear death and to avoid grief and we haven't known
how to approach and begin to make friends with these natural and normal
aspects of every human life. We haven't had the skills, the knowledge, or the
support to go beyond this culturally constructed aversion to death and the
fear of strong emotions that goes with it. An encounter with death breaks
open the heart and releases us from the confines of our personal story into
a new and unknown space, which may at times feel vast and unstructured,
scary and without comfort. In a culture stripped of any sense of the sacred
we are unable to trust ourselves to a journey into the unknown. And yet, it
is only by facing into death that we can discover our full humanity. And it
is only by fully embracing our human-ness that we can step into our destiny
as spiritual beings having a human experience.

As I felt into my brother's life I saw how his inability to grieve the many
losses and lacks of his life undermined his self-esteem, robbed him of his
creativity and created an environment for the health problems which were a
cause of his early death. It was this realisation that made me determined to
liberate death and grief from their cultural prison, to throw open the door
wide and allow in the light.

The journey of grief may at times feel unbearable as we are living it but
the consequences of not grieving are even more dangerous. As individuals,
avoidance of death and grief results in compromised lives. Collectively, it is

clear to see how turning a blind eye to death and grief – and in the process closing the heart and disconnecting from Soul – is the root cause of the inhumanity we can see so clearly demonstrated in our world. The extinction of species, the exploitation of our natural environment and the depletion of our natural resources, war, genocide and social inequality, the poisoning of life itself; all have their roots in our species' separation from soul life.

I'm presenting some very big concepts here but at the same time the process of transformation with which you and I can choose to co-operate, is present in quite mundane details of everyday life and it's important to hold both the big picture and the daily details in mind, For example, I've told several stories about how I noticed I was judging and closing my heart to my brother and how, as a consequence I was able to make new and different choices. Such changes may seem quite small and barely worth a mention, but this is how consciousness transforms – one person, one thought, one choice, one action, at a time.

It's also possible to notice collective trends within the process. For example, during the years I worked as a psychotherapist, as a teacher of psychotherapy and with leaders in the service professions, I met many hundreds of people in open and unguarded states, as they explored their inner experience. I noticed what appears to be a shared human trait: just as much as we want to live fully, we also resist life. Just as much as we strive to take care of ourselves and to be self-responsible and creative, for many of us a daily battle rages between self-love and self-neglect, between aspiration and inertia. I certainly know that conflict in myself. Do you? It appears to be at the heart of the human condition. You might call it our fatal flaw but this tendency towards entropy is also built into the universe. When we allow ourselves to feel it, this inner conflict can become the creative tension that will propel us forward and, as we resolve it within ourselves, we become active co-creators with conscious and cosmic evolution.

This conflict between the pull towards life and an opposing pull towards inertia and death, is something I witnessed in both Woods and David, as well as in myself. Woods knew he had cancerous cells a couple of years before he was given the final confirmation of impending death. In those two years, he drank a lot of delicious juices and took a heap of supplements, attempting to make his body more alkaline and bring it back into balance. Yet he didn't significantly change his standard American diet, ease off his intake of alcohol, or invest in a coach or healer who may have been able to help him add years to his life through healthy nutrition. The new behaviours were running alongside the old habits. I found it hard to challenge him about this because he was protective of what he regarded as his "freedom". Towards the end, when I suggested the large tankard of red wine he consumed on a nightly basis might not be the healthiest option, he responded that it was "all he had left". I'm sure the wine took the edge off his physical and psychological pain but I also suspect the intoxicants he had been using habitually all his life to lift himself and numb his pain, had robbed him of the power to fully feel, release and integrate his experience, and this limitation was a big contributor to the malfunctioning of his body. I had to face the probability that there was part of him that was ready to die and he'd had enough of human life. As I said goodbye to him, I needed to reach the place in my heart where I could accept his decision to leave me and release him from my attachment so that he could be free to pursue his own destiny. That was hard.

David too had many years of cigarette smoking and nightly consumption of wine and whisky in front of the tv, although he had effortlessly kicked these habits several years before his death. It was food that killed David and the stress of carrying many extra kilos of fat. He was addicted to sugar and, in the supermarket, would load up the trolley with cream cakes, biscuits, and chocolate bars which he ate late at night as comfort food before he went to bed.

Many times I have heard people say, "it's all I have left". These common addictions and eating disorders mask the quiet despair experienced by so many people in our western culture. Any substance dependency – whether it's alcohol, sugar, prescription or recreational drugs, disempowers by weakening the body's natural homeostasis and can prevent the underlying causes of pain from being thoroughly investigated and released. A roller coaster of highs and lows is substituted for true nourishment and, without true nourishment, it is difficult to take the actions that will change a life for the better and lead in the direction of our dreams.

This is what our culture of empty food and compensatory consumerism is doing to us. I have had my share of addictive and self-sabotaging patterns and I am not judgmental of my friend and my brother as I write this, I am simply reporting what I have witnessed. I feel a great sadness for the blindness with which we humans waste ourselves and try to drown our sorrows and I carry an angry incredulity at how the culture has colluded to keep us clinging to life-denying habits. Even Woods, who was otherwise a highly conscious man with an ecstatic love of life, could be blind to his own choices. And David, who so passionately wanted to build his eco-home, in the event, literally didn't have the heart for it. Hearts and lungs eventually give out under the strain of a lifetime's stifled grieving, strangled self-expression and disconnection from the source of healthy self-love.

What is it that makes us humans so ambivalent about living? We choose to deaden ourselves in so many ways. We want something badly – say, we want to get fit and healthy – and, on the surface, it seems all our efforts are moving in that direction, while all the time those old internal saboteurs that keep us from loving ourselves, are having a field day. We blow the diet or miss the yoga class, and then slide back into self-defeat. We simply don't show up 100% and we always have plenty of excuses. At the core of the conditioned human mind is the belief that we are not good enough, that we don't deserve, that we can't have what we long for; and so we're stuck with that story and keep proving it over and over. This is truly tragic and, as I see it, our biggest challenge as humans is to transform this tragedy into a new and different story.

I believe grieving consciously can be a gateway into a deep collective healing process which will give rise to a new consciousness and a new culture in harmony with life. In the following pages I will share with you some of my personal experience as I've moved through this transition to a more unified consciousness and I will offer skills that can help you to support yourself as you co-operate with the conscious healing process.

Transformation Means Letting Go of Who You Thought You Were

*The authentic self can only be fully realised when we are willing
to welcome every part of us, our shadows as well as our light.*

We can resist grief, or we can grieve partially, just enough to get by, but when we allow grief close, we will be changed by it. As you actively co-operate with the grieving process it becomes a process of transformation that will renew you if you let it. The process of renewal involves a falling away of some aspect of your personality which no longer serves you and your authentic purpose. For example, I had a friend with a wicked sense of humour. It was the first thing you noticed about her; she could see something funny in everything and she'd light up the room with her wry observations. Then, during the course of a big healing episode her sense of humour vanished and we saw the woman underneath the laughter was serious, stern and quite angry at times. She discovered she had been using humour all her life to cover unhealed wounds that still lived in her from childhood. Humour made her more attractive to others and was a good way to distract herself from her pain and hide those aspects of herself she didn't want to own. Now she had to endure the loss of this familiar way of connecting with people, get to know herself anew and give her childhood traumas some attention. This was an uncomfortable healing process which took time, courage and endurance. When the work was complete she was free to use humour appropriately.

We all develop personalities as faces to meet the world and we become identified with these partial versions of ourselves, thinking that's who we are. But we are more than this. During times of growth we have the opportunity to let go of anything that is false or limited so that our authenticity can shine through. I've been showing how, following the death of a family member, we have the chance to become aware of behaviour patterns which we have unconsciously developed over a lifetime. Nevertheless our old identities, and the behaviours we've learned in the family, have taken care of us in their own way and they are not so easily disposed of. You may feel quite shaken and lost as the habitual layers of your thinking and behaviour start to fall away. This shifting of identity can be just as disconcerting as the loss of your loved one and can be experienced as a little death of the self. It isn't only your limitations that are revealed, your strengths too may have been in hiding and appear now from out of the shadows to be celebrated and to find expression. This too will change and challenge you. You will need to draw on all your inner resources as you hold yourself through these inner revolutions.

During this time of the dying away of the self, no matter how much personal work you have done, you will often feel like a beginner and be taken by surprise and thrown off your familiar perch into the unknown, where you flounder. This uncertainty is unnerving and will cause you to doubt yourself, sometimes radically, but this is where the transformational power of healing lies. I want to reassurance you that if this is happening to you, there is nothing wrong with you and you are not going mad. This is a process which can renew you. Healing, when given all the necessary space and entered into deeply, can be a rite of passage which takes you through deathliness to new life and an expanded consciousness. Having a map of the territory and developing a few simple skills will help you to navigate through the healing process more easily. Finding a tribe of like-minded people who are travelling through similar deep-sea changes will also ease your passage. In these very troubled times in which we live, none of us can do this alone, we all need each other. Together we can create more expanded fields of consciousness to lift us all.

When you are willing to shed inflexible and limiting ideas of who you are you open to the possibility to start a new chapter of your individual life story *and* to allow a new human story to emerge through you. In the act of sitting with the death of the old, your love, understanding and compassion for what it is to be human will deepen. You will expand your possibilities as you consciously choose to be a creative and wholehearted participant in life.

You may feel uncomfortable considering the notion that grieving can lead to joy and fulfilment and that you can be of service to humanity in this way. Perhaps you simply want your pain to go away and I sympathise with that wish. When I entered my period of deep healing, I had been on a conscious spiritual path for twenty-five years and I'd gathered many tools and practices for calming the mind and emotions but at that time all my tools, and the more expansive spiritual perspectives I usually lived within, eluded me. This created an experience of entrapment, flatness and no escape, in which I felt reduced to a single focus and without my usual powers and resilience. In time, I would remember that what I saw as emptiness is actually a source of love, alive with possibilities and full of gifts. But, numb with shock, I couldn't connect with my wisdom.

There are many reasons why we shun the deeper dive of grief – distrust of the inner world, fear of being judged, busy crowded lives, not having the skills, experience or understanding for grieving fully. Even amongst those of us who are on a conscious healing path and want to know ourselves better there is an innate tendency within the human mind to hide from self-awareness and to avoid full self-responsibility. The tendency to want to preserve the illusion that we are more conscious, more loving, more special, more virtuous, or more self-realised than we are, is common. We desire to live only in the light, to deny the shadowy aspects of human behaviour, and we avoid experiencing our full, complex humanity, including all the messy bits. Unfortunately, when we avoid our hidden rage, our veiled despair, the shame and guilt that lie beneath the surface of everyday life, or we remain unconscious of our mean-spiritedness, manipulative behaviours and our failures to take responsibility for our gifts, we cut ourselves off from the true power of the authentic self and deny ourselves the chance to blossom into our full potential. Yes, I am saying that the authentic self can only be fully realised when we are willing to welcome every part of us, those parts that live in the shadows as well as those that live in the light.

As conscious healers we need to be willing to do whatever it takes to move through the dying of the old self until we reach the new. And it takes as long as it takes. The healing process is an engagement with an intelligent life force or evolutionary impulse which moves through us and with which we can learn to co-operate skilfully, with awareness, wisdom and choice. The transformational process keeps evolving and there's always more to learn and this makes it ever fascinating and exciting when approached with curiosity and an open mind.

One of the most important skills of conscious healing is to set an intention which will guide the process and keep you on track. My intention on that chilly April day was to see past my dread and use the situation I was in to heal myself and to evolve consciously. That is the choice I made and, in doing so, I brought my will into line with the deeper truth of Soul and became an active participant in the process of healing and renewal. Be aware that when you do this everything that is not yet aligned with your intention will show up to be seen. You may feel worse before you feel better and you will surely be stretched beyond whatever you felt you were capable of. Being present with your experience, suspending judgments and being kind to yourself, is the most constructive approach.

A Bigger Perspective Will Support and Motivate You Through the Hardest Times

> *Because I know all life is interconnected as one living organism,*
> *to do anything other than live from my wholeness makes no sense.*
> *I am not separate from the world; I am in it and of it.*

The challenges of the transformational process are such that it helps enormously to have a philosophy which provides a bigger picture. In fact it's not possible to become an active co-operator with the transformational process unless you have a more expansive context to support you. We need a strong reason to keep making the heroic attempt to free ourselves from the weight of history and cultural conditioning and to live from our authentic values. Even with a higher perspective, it is possible to fall back into individualistic thinking and mistake the pains of transformation for a sign that "we have done something wrong" and "this is all about me". Such thoughts keep us stuck. The bigger perspective that can support us may be a historical-cultural perspective, a global perspective or a spiritual or universal perspective, for example.

The philosophy I have been drawn to is that I am a spiritual being here on Earth with the opportunity to fully experience all that it means to be human, whilst at the same time remembering the true, essential, timeless being that I am. This philosophy goes hand in hand with the practice of living consciously and the art of valuing and balancing both my human and my spiritual existence, and ultimately bringing these into harmony and co-operation. This is quite a stretch and a balancing act. I need to be open to experience all the messiness of being human - all the conflicts, mistakes, failures, disappointments and suffering – and at the same time create the best conditions for experiencing the joy, peace, love, freedom and inspiration of spiritual being - whilst not getting attached to any of it or identifying too much with any passing state. This is quite an art!

My philosophy has evolved over a lifetime and I will tell you how in the next chapter. It's not an abstract teaching I have swallowed down whole but a living eco-system of inner knowing and experience that has been revealed to me bit by bit and then grown within me. For example, the understanding that all of life is inter-connected and inter-dependent, started as an interesting idea which I was curious about but didn't fully understand. It took some years before I came to know it with my heart, and that was the crucial step. The shift in consciousness I'm talking about here is from the illusion of separation, which is a mental construct, to the knowing of unity within the heart. As human beings we have been conditioned to feel separate from each other and from life. As spiritual beings we know All is One. When I remember I am connected to everything, I know my state of consciousness and energy make a difference to the bigger wholes of which I am part and any healing I do is not just for my own personal benefit. I'm motivated by a longing to be the healthiest cell I can be in the organism of humanity and of life itself, to be a force for positive change rather than part of the world's problems. Because I know all life is interconnected in one living organism, to do anything other than live from my wholeness makes no sense. I am not separate from the world; I am in it and of it.

Occasionally, when I am going through a major transition, such as the one I'm telling you about now, I question even my most cherished understandings. I think it's healthy to do so even though it may shake my foundations at the time. But mostly, my philosophy is the ground from which I live, it's what gets me out of bed in the morning and informs my choices every day.

Identifying as a soul is crucial to my willingness to submit to the labour pains of evolving consciously. We all have conditioned minds and sensitive emotional bodies but the soul lives outside time in a multidimensional reality that connects us to a greater meaning and belonging. When I am in the grip of strong emotion I may be conflicted, confused or hurting but, as soon as I step into the perspective of this expanded, intelligent, interconnected consciousness and remember I am a soul with a bigger destiny, within a much bigger story, any personal pain is eased.

Death invites us into this transformational opportunity to embrace both our human and our spiritual aspects and bring them into harmony. Every death that touches us is an opportunity to experience both the human and the spiritual aspects of our being and to bring the separated human aspects more fully into balance with the expansive, unconditional love of Soul. This is why it is so important for those of us on a conscious path to give the healing process all the time it requires. Grief clears away everyday distractions and opens the heart so that we can more easily access this deeper wisdom. We may connect with this reality most easily when we are still, silent, present, focused, listening and intentional, or in a creative act such as writing.

As with most other worthwhile things in life we learn to grieve by grieving and we learn to heal by healing. Like the serpentine water monster in Greek mythology, the Hydra, loss is a beast with many heads. Each time you cut off a head, another one grows in its place.

So here I am, walking through life, doing my best to hold all my human complexity alongside my spiritual nature. When I remember my spiritual nature and the bigger story, I gather strength to keep enduring and moving through the emotional pain and discomfort of being a human in a transformational process at a crucial time.

Questions for Inquiry

Questions of identity can help to unlock the transformational potential that lies within grief.

Death poses the questions:
Who are you?
Who are you in relation to death?

Who are you in relation to life?

What is a human life for?

How will you choose to live today?

Take one question each day, as a living inquiry and carry it with you throughout the day. In the evening, or the following morning, settle into a receptive frame of mind and explore your answers to the question through writing or drawing.

Chapter Three

Soul Work

The Soul Journey

> *Personal grief can open a doorway into the transpersonal process*
> *of conscious healing through which we come to see that we are each*
> *a fractal of a greater whole and each individual's story resonates*
> *within a common, shared humanity. As we sense into the essential*
> *interconnectedness, or inter-being, of humanity and all other life forms,*
> *forgiveness, self-forgiveness and compassion naturally arise. Tending*
> *the fires of the broken heart changes the world for the better.*

Over the course of my lifetime I've come to see in every human life the potential for a heroic journey of liberation from all the forces that seek to keep us small and confined. It's a journey to liberate our unique gifts – our creative genius, our authenticity, our wisdom and our love - so that we can find fulfilment by being of service. Each of us has unique gifts and a unique niche within a co-creative cosmos and it's a matter of finding our gifts, allowing ourselves to have them, and committing to use them for the common good.

I have lived this journey and developed my understanding of it throughout my lifetime and I've found various tools and pathways to support me. This started when I engaged with the Women's Liberation Movement in my 20's. Then in my 30's I became involved in psychotherapy and group work. Meditation and spiritual practice followed in my 40's; evolutionary spirituality and the process of transformation in my 50's and 60's. Now, I understand this journey of liberation is a path of conscious healing and giving grief all the time and attention it needs is a vital part of the process.

We are all at some stage of the Soul Journey but the deeper process of conscious healing, is not something everyone experiences. At this particular moment of history, when our whole world is in a transition of consciousness, many of us have taken on the labour of conscious healing as our soul work - a way to clear old paradigm values from our system and, in so doing, to lift consciousness on the planet. I believe it is only through this inner process of transformation that we humans will change sufficiently to ensure our survival as a species and this belief motivates all the work I do.

The new culture aligned with life, which we so desperately need worldwide, can only be built from a state of inner wholeness. This will only come about as those of us called to do so are willing to take deep dives into the shadows of our own humanity, to find compassion, and embody a new compassionate culture within our own hearts and minds, and with each other in community. When grief feels too difficult or painful and we seek to avoid or repress it, we interrupt the process of transformation and cannot embody our essential wholeness. By sharing my own experiences I am attempting to bring the more intense experiences of conscious healing into the light and to provide encouragement and support for those of you who are experiencing something similar. I want you to know you are not alone and that grieving and healing, however harrowing, are normal and inevitable aspects of human experience and can become the fertile ground from which new life grows.

As I grieved for my brother, I realised grief has been with me, in one form or another, all my life. As a sensitive, caring empath I took the pain of my family members into my own being with no sense of where I ended and they began. When my parents were fighting I sat upstairs in bed, or on the stairs, contracted with anxiety, thinking it was all my fault and I had to fix it, yet having no idea what I could do to help. Over time, my fear and helplessness combined with a seething sense of injustice at my father's domination of my mother and brother and gave rise to an exaggerated sense of responsibility, which became both a burden I carried and a strong motivational force. It has taken a lifetime to make sense of the suffering in my little family unit and to release my judgments, so that I can see the family as a microcosm of the human story, rather than as proof of my personal unworthiness, and find peace with it all.

I have realised more deeply than before that healing the world takes place within me and it is in my most personal relationships that I am most challenged. I have remembered that I can't change what happens *to* me but I can have control over *how* I respond to life's hardships and it is in these daily, moment to moment choices that freedom lies. The practice of conscious healing constantly brings me into a state of humility and self-forgiveness as I frequently fail to live up to my values. As we make the choice to heal we can deconstruct our cultural conditioning – all those messages that we are "not good enough", "not worthy", that our inner knowing is "heresy" that our creativity and inner authority are "dangerous", that the troubles of the world are "all our fault". This cultural conditioning, that keeps us stuck in limitation and lack, goes deep and has kept people captive for centuries. It is truly life-changing to allow our unconscious patterns of thought and behaviour to rise into awareness and then choose to liberate ourselves from them.

The Life Review as a Tool for Transformation

> *The power of this process of coming to peace with our personal history should not be underestimated. It is only through fully knowing our own woundedness and our own creative genius that we can grasp the scope of the human condition. Then we can live compassionately, in service to liberating humanity from the crushing weight of the past.*

When we choose to sit with our grief as part of a conscious healing practice, in the ways I am describing, opportunities for transformation arise. At the centre of the process of transformation and liberation is the power of choice. We make many choices every day; some of these are unconscious choices driven by habit; some are conscious choices that support well-being, creativity and the quality of our relationships. We also make choices at a soul level which we are not always aware of but which guide our lives. For example, my decision to follow the path of becoming a conscious healer was a soul choice, and my decision to return to the UK to support my brother was a consequence of that choice. By bringing our soul choices into conscious awareness we can empower ourselves to come into alignment with our deepest purpose and take daily actions which support what is most important to us.

Most of the literature exploring what happens when we die, speaks of a life review shortly after spirit is released from the body. This event is said to occur all at once, holographically, within seconds of Earth time. We are shown all the events of our lifetime: all the choices we have made and the consequences of these choices; how our actions have affected others; and how we have fulfilled, or not, our own soul potential and destiny.

We don't have to wait to die before we complete a life review. For me, perhaps because of my interest in the bigger meaning of life and my desire to understand human psychology, partial life reviews have arisen naturally at key crisis and transition points, as an ongoing way to digest and integrate my life experience and take my bearings on the Soul Journey. Life review is part of a slow and steady movement towards realising our authentic truth and essential being. Memories of life events simply arise spontaneously, like a movie, to be looked at and felt into. I think of it as a chance to chew over the memories and any emotional residue I'm carrying so that I can extract the life-giving juices and discard what is no longer true or helpful.

Inevitably, grieving for my brother stimulated a life review. Although previously, I had reached an understanding and acceptance of my life story, I was now called to go around again and take a fresh look. I saw how, from my soul's perspective, my life had unfolded in three 22-year chapters and that these chapters map the evolutionary process of my Soul Journey. (If a 22-year cycle doesn't ring true for you, please bear with me. When I was speaking with a friend recently, she immediately identified her life chapters as being a sixteen-year cycle. Each one of us is different and I offer some guidance for identifying your soul chapters at the end of this chapter.)

I'm going to explore this process of life review in some depth using my own life as an example. One of the things I hope you will get from this is the realisation that although each of our life stories is unique, we all grow from the earth of a common humanity. There is no one else quite like you, nor has there ever been, nor ever will be. You have been born here on Earth with a particular set of gifts and challenges and you have a unique and necessary role to play in the eco-system of life. At the same time, we are all embedded in a particular cultural and historical context and we are carried by the stream of consciousness available in our particular epoch. To a large extent we can't move faster than this stream but as we play our part we help the stream to move and evolve, just as it carries us.

As you consider the life review, please hold these threads of perspective together:

+ You are a soul with a unique destiny which unfolds throughout your lifetime and through many lifetimes;
+ You are an inseparable part of a historical and cultural movement through which humanity is slowly awakening to its bigger destiny;
+ The bigger story of our species Soul is an evolutionary imperative that holds within it the potential liberation of humanity from suffering and the consequent creation of peaceful and harmonious co-existence here on Earth and within the bigger dance of Cosmos;
+ You always have a choice who you are in relation to this movement of awakening and you can choose to live consciously and with the intention to co-operate with this potential unfolding;
+ In our present story on Earth, when there is so much upheaval, inequality and suffering, it can be difficult to keep sight of this bigger, hopeful picture.

I believe the only way we will get through these very troubled times and survive as a species is by remembering the wholeness of who we are and why we are here. Even when life appears to be eclipsed by sorrow, and we are in despair, we can keep choosing to align with this bigger purpose. This is the soul work of the conscious healer.

Holding Creative Tension

There is something bigger than self-interest moving us towards liberation.
An evolutionary impulse inherent in the universe moves through each
of us, shaking us awake and calling us to live fully and to evolve.

Our soul choices exist in tension with our cultural conditioning and this has the potential to propel us towards liberation. The foundations of personal psychology are created through the conditioning received within the family, within the education system and societal influences at large - for example our conditioning as a woman or a man, the culture in which we grew up, our race and the colour of our skin. This is the clay we work with during a lifetime. You could call this **the cultural thesis.** The personal journey towards liberation and expanded consciousness, guided by Soul, is **the antithesis** through which we discover who we are authentically.

These two opposing forces in the psyche – the cultural conditioning of the personality versus authentic individual self-expression guided by the multi-dimensional soul – create an inner tension which can lead to important choices. Within the tension between the deeply engrained limitations of family patterns and cultural conditions, on the one hand, and the creative aspirations of the soul, which directs and motivates our deepest learning and highest values, on the other, arise our unique gifts for self-expression and our vehicles for serving life. In other words, there is something bigger than self-interest moving us towards liberation. An evolutionary impulse inherent in the universe moves through each of us, shaking us awake and calling us to live fully and to evolve. Gradually, with time and commitment, we can free ourselves from the restrictions which limit our fullest expression.

I offer some of my own life story to illustrate how this Soul Journey can unfold through the lifetime.

Soul Chapter One: Childhood, Family and the Cultural Thesis

My brother's death and the writing of this book are showing me more and more clearly how my family provided the training ground for my initiation into the soul work of conscious healing. My family were the perfect people with whom I could learn the lessons I needed, both for my own liberation and so that I could make my contribution to the wellbeing and empowerment of others. The container my family provided gave me the essential physical nurturance that enabled me to grow, yet the environment was emotionally toxic and oppressive to my spirit and so it also afforded a strong drive towards freedom. As children, my brother and I lived within the battlefield of our parent's fights and this fired in me a fierce determination to free myself from what I experienced as a form of psychic imprisonment. I also had a deep longing to free my mother. As I became an adult and began my work in the world I was drawn to work with women, first focusing on my own liberation and empowerment and then passing on whatever I was learning to others through my various professional roles as educator, gestalt therapist and change-agent. Later this desire to help others liberate themselves extended to my father and my brother and this provided me with further opportunities to open my heart and become more skilful.

As a child, I learned how to take care of myself and to bide my time as the seed of my unique calling grew within its shell, fulfilling the timing of its own DNA. Yet the trauma I experienced within the family environment had long term consequences for me. I was seven years old when I realised my parents were not able to give me the nurturance I needed to grow authentically and I made a decision at a soul level (I certainly could not have expressed this in words at the time) to preserve my own integrity and autonomy as best I could. I followed this decision by spending as much time as I could away from home. I found a friend with a stable, happy family who generously opened their home to me and welcomed me to their table, where I comforted myself with sweet food. When I was nine years old my family moved to a new home in a new town. Separated from my best friend, the local state school where I had been a playground leader, and the familiarity of the village, I took refuge in my imagination. Reading adventure stories and writing my own stories became the safe space where I could wrap a cocoon around myself and escape into freedom.

For a while after our move to the new house Dad was much more open, happy and expansive and it seemed we were making a new start as a family. With no best friend and nowhere to run to, I moved closer to him. I was excited when he arrived home from work and I'd chatter away to him and engage him in conversation which he appeared to enjoy. But then, that Christmas, as we were about to sit down to our Christmas dinner, he was overcome by a violent explosion of rage. I don't remember much more about this event as a dark curtain descended within me and I retreated into myself in fear. It wasn't until I was in my fifties, when I went to take care of Dad after Mum died, that I was able to look beneath the fear and realise how traumatised I had been by this unprovoked and ugly explosion of rage. Age nine, in that moment of recoil from his rage, I became split inside. I explored this split and the effect it had on my autonomy in my book, *Migration to the Heartland:* [1]

> Walking today through the bush, feeling as always its ancient being, suddenly a shaft of sunlight fell through the trees, and I started to identify with my soul.
>
> I have been thinking about my father from whom I've been estranged for many years. His rejection of me as a child gave rise to fear, hurt and shame and this has been a major contributor to my core sense of unworthiness, feeding the inner monster of doubt. I know it's time now to cut the cords, end my attachment, and let go of the old story.
>
> When I was a child, he was my daddy and I his special girl. But that feeling of specialness was difficult to reconcile with his unpredictable temper and the way he dominated my mother. So I split my daddy and myself in two. "Good Daddy" was generous, handsome and committed to the well-being of his family. He provided treats and holidays and schooling, working hard for us all. "Bad Daddy" was a harsh tyrant who demanded obedience to his will.

"Good girl" was bright, achieving, a lively and confident companion, basking in approval. "Bad girl" was anxious, guilty, rebellious and full of rage. My father's angry outbursts always came as a shock to me; I knew I was being found "wrong" but never knew my crime. I came to believe any unhappiness in the family was all my fault and I had to find a way to put it right. I shouldered this burden of guilt and responsibility and carried it for my family.

As I grew into adolescence I became a silent rebel, passionately opposing my father's control inside myself while being externally compliant. I would not surrender my autonomy in order to keep my father's love; it was too high a price to pay. His conditional love, dependent on my conforming to his expectations for a good daughter and a good woman, felt increasingly like a prison from which I had to escape.

But whilst I rejected my father I still longed for his acceptance and felt incomplete without it. As a child I had his love and then lost it, a fall from grace which coincided in my mind with becoming a woman. So could I now be a woman and be lovable? More than that, could I be an autonomous woman with my own ideas, passions and direction and be lovable? It didn't seem possible. If I chose love I'd have to sacrifice parts of myself, and if I chose to be fully myself then I'd have to sacrifice love.

I am including these memories because I think it is important to point out that trauma doesn't necessarily have an obvious cause and yet it can have lifelong consequences. My father didn't hit or sexually abuse me but the force of his rage was an assault on my energy body and, what I felt as his sudden unprovoked abandonment of me, was enough to cause shame. This inner split in my psyche had marked effects on my self-esteem, on my future relationships with men and on my ability to risk full self-expression; limitations I have had to work with all my life.

In addition to these disappointments at home, from this point on, the formal education I received failed to nourish me and instead became a litany of humiliations and mind-numbing boredom. When I was nine, my parents sent me to a posh private school where I had to wear a school uniform including a hat that I hated because I felt it marked me out as different to the other kids in the street and helped to isolate me. At eleven I passed the 11+ exam with flying colours. This was an exam based on IQ, which everyone had to sit, and the results divided us into potential academic achievers who went on to Grammar schools and the technically oriented who went to Secondary Modern schools. Clearly, I was intellectually bright at the time and I was rewarded with a free place at a girls' school reputed to be the best in the region. But I found the education there just as boring, stifling and humiliating as at the previous school. Only friendships and dancing to the music of the Beatles got me through those years. At home I hid myself away behind piles of homework and became mute; with my friends I was a giggly, scruffy teenager; inside I was repressed and rebellious. From the age of twelve until I was twenty-nine I under-achieved academically. The trauma and shame I experienced at home, combined with the unimaginative, facts-based school curriculum, dulled my light.

My story isn't unusual. In post-war Britain we were living through a social revolution and a mass awakening that divided the generations. I had freedoms my parents had never known, not least a university education, and it must have been difficult for them to see how the aspirations they held for me were carrying me away from them. My father's driving ambition was to transcend the poverty in which he'd been raised but tragically moving into the comfortable middle class separated him from his roots in family and community and left my parents isolated. Watching them, I rejected material comfort as a stultifying selling of the soul and chose a life path of restlessness and spiritual adventure instead.

Another important thread of these childhood years was a realisation of trauma on a bigger scale through the threat to life on Earth posed by human conflict and division. The Cuban Missile crisis in 1962, when I was thirteen, was widely considered to be the closest the world came to full scale nuclear war during the Cold War between the United States and the Soviet Union. It was deeply chilling to my teenage mind and heart when I projected the distorted rage I had seen on my father's face onto a global screen and saw cold, grey-suited men sitting with fingers poised over the button that could release nuclear weapons and annihilate me, my family and much of life on Earth. I experienced this threat as a blight on my burgeoning young womanhood. How could I grow up to be whole and happy in a world so divided that life itself was under threat? This question has lived in me for a lifetime.

Within the stifling atmospheres of family and school I always knew there was something more and better and, if I could survive these years, I would then be free to go out and find it. When I was nineteen I began to awaken spiritually and to have glimpses of this "something more". I was reading English Literature at university and, on a cold, snowy April day, I read T.S. Eliot's, *Four Quartets*.[2] I wasn't yet emotionally or spiritually mature enough to fully understand the poem but it spoke directly to my soul and filled me with awe. At the same time an appreciation of beauty opened within me and the classic novels I was reading developed my empathy. I fell in love and, with my new best friend, discovered the joys of walking for days through the varied landscapes of the British Isles. My consciousness and my being were opening and expanding.

As I reflect on this first chapter of my life I am struck by the resilience and instinct for survival which I'm sure most children have – a determination to live, no matter what. We find creative ways to adapt to difficult situations and, even though we may be traumatised and wounded, there is something within us that stays pure and innocent; an innate wisdom and knowing that there's something more and better. Over time I could see that same innocence in all my family members too, even though it was often eclipsed. When I look back at that little girl who decided to take care of herself and then found and created safe spaces where she could sit out the storm, I am touched by her courage. My creative adaptations - taking refuge in books, in the imagination, in introspection - continued throughout my life to provide a safe growing space, my sanctuary. The damaged relationship with my father became a driving motivation to find, live from, and express my authentic self. Love and care for my mother became the motivation to liberate myself as a woman from the oppression of limiting patriarchal views and behaviours, and then to help other women to liberate themselves. And all of this was held within the global story of the battle between good and evil and the ever-impending threat of destruction which became a major source of motivation to empower myself to make a creative contribution. Everything to come was already there in that seven-year-old girl who made a decision to preserve her integrity by withdrawing from her family and taking care of herself as best she could. Even though this beginning led on to great adventures, I hold sorrow too for the lonely path of the orphaned girl carrying her burden of responsibility.

Soul Chapter Two: Young Adulthood, Individuation and Creative Expression

In my second soul chapter, from age 22 to 44, I began to separate from my family, physically and psychologically and to express myself as a unique individual. This is the process the great psychologist, C.G. Jung, called individuation, and it continues throughout a lifetime. For me, this chapter was a joyous leap into freedom after being confined in the stuffy, oppressive rooms of home and school. It wasn't all easy going by any means, there were big challenges along the way and I suffered some major disappointments, but the overall themes of this chapter were excitement, adventure, discovery and expansion.

One of the signs the soul path is activated, even when we don't consciously know it, is that synchronicities and serendipitous opportunities arise, and if we are alert, what we are seeking seems to fall effortlessly into our lap. For example, I didn't consciously choose to be a teacher, the careers officer at my university told me it was the best choice available to me and I somewhat reluctantly followed his advice. Later, I discovered teaching was a vital thread of my vocation. A few years after that, when I wanted to make the move from teaching into becoming a psychotherapist, I picked up the paper one day - which I very rarely did - and there was the perfect job for me, as a teacher in a family and child psychiatric unit, very close to where I lived. I applied for the position and was offered it. This in turn, a couple of years down the track, led to an unlooked for offer of a one year fully paid further training in Edinburgh, a city where I'd dreamed of living. This serendipitous move then opened the opportunity for me to train as a gestalt therapist and brought many new adventures and relationships that deepened my journey towards authenticity.

This second 22-year chapter was a playground for action and experimentation. In my early 20's, the second wave of the Women's Liberation Movement broke upon our shores and ignited in me a keen interest in psychology, feminism and personal empowerment. I joined feminist consciousness-raising groups, took up the mantra "the personal is political", participated in Women's Liberation conferences and was active in raising funds to create safe spaces for women and children at risk of domestic abuse. Later I undertook research into women and unemployment, as a result of which a women's training centre was opened in Edinburgh. I was a member of a women's writers group for several years and we published our own poetry. At the same time I feasted on books by feminist writers who were unashamedly breaking new ground by leaving old stereotypes behind and stepping into being a whole new kind of woman – unadorned, radical, intellectually brilliant and challenging. Some of the books I read were by Jungian feminists and it was Jung who first wrote about the Feminine and Masculine principles within the psyche. This gave me a language and ignited a strong desire, already latent in me, to redeem the creative Feminine from the tyranny of the dominating Masculine, within myself, through the work I did with other women, and in the wider world.

Cultural change was underway and it provided a heady mix of new, life-changing ideas. The transition of humanity, from the old life-threatening cultural paradigm to a new life-affirming paradigm and culture, had begun. Radical commentary emerged from the field of mental health through writer and psychiatrist R.D. Laing and his book *The Divided Self*.[3] Theodore Roszak in *The Making of the Counter Culture*[4] was another of many authors who revealed me to myself in new and exciting ways. By analysing culture and society they were saying, this is where you've come from, this is what's really going on, this is who you could be. It was all intensely stimulating and I can still remember where I was the day I set eyes on my first feminist book, *Sexual Politics* by Kate Millett[5] in 1970, or Marilyn Ferguson's, *The Aquarian Conspiracy* in 1980,[6] or Stan Grof's, *Spiritual Emergence* in 1989.[7] I can still smell the clean new pages of a book of poems by my favourite poet, Adrienne Rich, *A Wild Patience Has Taken Me This Far*,[8] as I stood at a bus stop taking my first peek into the new world of radical authenticity she was opening up for me. Those years, from the early 1970's right through to the present day, have been an exhilarating explosion of creativity and new ways of thinking, seeding a new culture and pointing the way towards a better future. I feel immensely privileged to have been here as a witness and participant and, in the midst of it all, to have found my soul path, my own individual meaning and purpose.

Our collective journey towards liberation, expanded consciousness, protest and creativity was thrilling and sometimes great fun, but it was not easy. By the early 80's it was becoming apparent to me and my feminist sisters that our tools, along with our growing cultural analysis, were not enough. Untamed ego was rampant within and between us and our energy became dissipated as we turned against each other, unable to accept our differences. We soon realized ideas alone were not enough and if we wanted to change the world we needed to raise our consciousness and then embody and live the change. Many of us began to seek out the many forms of psychotherapy and intense experiential learning groups which were suddenly available everywhere. A treasure trove of healing modalities and therapies appeared alongside spiritual practices and traditions. Some of these were ancient practices that had been well loved in the past and then repressed and forgotten, others evolved out of new psychological understandings. It was only when we started to use these tools to look inwards that we discovered just how deeply and tenaciously the old, life-denying culture had taken root inside us.

A compelling need to heal, liberate and make whole what has been fragmented, damaged and wasted, naturally led me to explore the inner world. My inner journey began with spontaneous inner awakenings and the arising of poetry into my life. I was twenty-nine and living alone for the first time after leaving an eight-year relationship. For a year prior to this I had been experiencing an uncomfortable build-up of energy which felt like being in a pressure cooker. I attempted to relieve this desperate feeling of entrapment with alcohol, wild dancing and sex. As a naturally shy person, the alcohol loosened my inhibitions, I danced to reach out and break the chains that bound me, and sex afforded me brief moments of bodily ecstasy and closeness that released me from the confines of lonely individuality.

Yet these attempts at release didn't bring me any lasting relief and were frequently followed by depression.

I had no language for the inner world at that time. If someone had asked me how I felt – and I don't think anyone ever did – I would have struggled to put a sentence together. I was living from the surface of myself, driven by emotions and urges I did not understand or reflect upon. From my present-day perspective I would say I was unconscious – intellectually bright but lacking in the awareness and wisdom that enables any depth of self-reflection and deliberate choice. In other words, I wasn't guiding and shaping my own destiny but simply reacting to whatever was put in front of me.

When I could no longer bear my intense discomfort, I had no idea what else to do but to leave the relationship and the party life at the university where my partner taught. I effortlessly found the first of many shabby rural cottages which became my natural habitat. My partner had been my best friend for eight years and, in leaving him, I felt a devastating loss, disappointment and sense of failure. Being in the world alone for the first time scared me and I spent much of the next four months, lying on the earth outside my cottage, crying out my grief.

Then, when my grieving for the relationship was over, a new spaciousness opened up. When I got home from work in the afternoon, I began to sit quietly in the living room with a pen and notebook and poems spontaneously started to flow through me. It was as if a lively stream of wisdom had been waiting for its time to be released so that it could ripple across the paper and show me who I really am.

The poems astonished me because I didn't think them up, they simply showed up, fully formed. They spoke in a different voice to my everyday personality; a wise and authoritative, authentic voice far wiser than me. I was thrilled - and that is one of the primary characteristics of creating - excitement lifts me out of the mundane repetitions and frustrations of daily life into a transcendent realm which is always new, unexpected and surprising. Excitement is a mobilisation of energy which becomes a momentum the more I give it my attention. It wasn't only the artefacts of the poems that delighted me – the fact that I had created something out of nothing, something that would last – it was the discovery of a whole new dimension of being I hadn't previously known existed. When my inner world revealed itself in this way, I found an Aladdin's cave; a magical, mystical world of endless riches and possibility. And this was very compelling.

This opening into my inner world made me more intelligent, capable and confident in the outer world too. I had been underachieving since the age of twelve. In the face of problems at home and tedium at school, my intelligence had gone underground, like a bulb patiently awaiting the right season to bloom. When the time was right, my petals effortlessly opened to reveal the poetry and magic hidden in my soul.

A deeper self was communicating with me through poetry, and the solitary, rural life I'd chosen gave me the space, stillness and silence in which I could concentrate on the practice of listening deeply. This came naturally to me, as if I was already skilled at it. As a personality I was frequently inarticulate, full of self-doubt, lacking in confidence and confused, yet the poet's voice was strong, knowing, powerful and mature. Where was this voice coming from? How could these two totally different beings – the immature, unconscious personality and the wise, knowing author, inhabit one body?

> The poems were like a language from another world. I felt someone was trying to communicate with me urgently and it was important to understand. I was in a state of creative ferment, catching lines of poetry like glittering fishes on the end of my line, reeling them in, savouring them. When a poem was complete, I'd read it again and again; each one felt precious. I ran around showing them to anyone who would listen, saying, "Look what I've made…"
>
> Writing poetry is like entering another dimension of experience, beyond this material world, these physical senses. At the beginning it was a new world, mysterious and very exciting, which I entered like an archaeologist or a geologist, scraping away the dirt from an artefact, hammering out little compacted word gems from the rock face. Even though I didn't fully understand their cryptic

messages, I knew they were signposts into an uncharted realm. Listening for poems was my way of slipping through the cracks between the worlds, and I felt compelled to go to this other world with its new language as often as I could. It was many years before I realized the one who was trying to communicate with me was my own soul." [9]

A door had swung open into a whole new dimension of being. I was bowled over by awe and wonder and the activities of daily life paled in comparison. Later I came to understand this as an opening to the spiritual dimension within me through which my soul was emerging to be heard. Writing poetry enabled me to focus the intense energy of this spiritual awakening and became a boat to carry me through the turbulent seas of the following years. When I look at a photograph of myself at that time I see the person I would continue to be, essentially, for the rest of my life.

In order to receive the riches of the authentic self, I'd sacrificed a relationship and an old identity which had grown too confining. In writing poetry I found the thing I cared about enough to give it my time, energy and passion and it became my vehicle for the unfolding journey of my soul. Through developing this practice of deep inner listening I grew my skills and developed understanding. I also discovered my motivation to master the creative process, a practice that would continue to fascinate me for the rest of my life. I learned early on that to earn the satisfaction of creating I have to be prepared to do whatever it takes and that isn't always what I would prefer or even what seems rational. When I take up my pen, I put myself in service to an intelligence much bigger than me - the wisdom of soul with its longing for conscious experience - and the evolutionary impulse, the spirit-in-action which flows through soul and calls me to be its hands and eyes and voice. This being- in-service to something much bigger stretches me, exercises my mind and brings me joy.

Writing poetry led me into an exploration of the inner world where I became an archaeologist of Soul. At that time I had no idea what Soul was and even my use of the word came later. Through reaching for the images of poetry I patiently uncovered bit by bit multi-coloured patterns of a mosaic that lies beneath the covering of earth and history. I came to realise that the oppression of women is just one version of cultural colonisation and, at the root of all oppression, is the suppression of Soul. Throughout history, we, the People, have been robbed of our connection to Soul by empire and army, church and state, industry and commerce, whose minions have been practiced at subduing individual and collective self-expression and indigenous, soul-based culture in order to serve their interests. The current desecration of life on the planet and the global cauldron of inequality, social injustice and violence in which we live today are, in my view, the result of this separation from Soul life. This is the tragedy in which we are all embroiled. Writing poetry opened a doorway into an exploration of Soul and awoke within me an inner reservoir of wisdom, creative potential and a longing to heal, which then directed and guided me and gave my life meaning, even in the hardest times.

During this second soul chapter a shy, self-doubting and unconfident young woman transformed into a teacher, a gestalt therapist, a leader, an entrepreneur, an innovator, a community developer, a poet, a feminist and a student of soul. Where did all that come from? There were no precedents in my family for these roles, so I guess they are the seeds of the wisdom and potential I brought with me as the treasure and growing shoots of my soul. As I followed the presenting opportunities my life was filled with relationships, fun, having a home, being out in nature, exploring culture, and inner work. To be sure I was a wounded healer and frequently heartbroken but I was fully alive, passionate and self-actualising.

In my early 30's I began an adventure that has lasted, in one form or another, for the rest of my life when I joined a training to become a gestalt therapist. Through the practice of gestalt therapy, I became a professional witness to the ways our life force can become tied up in knots and a guide to help people find their way out of the labyrinths of sorrow and suffering. I sat with others in grief and with my own seemingly unending river of tears. But it wasn't grief that drew me into gestalt therapy, it was excitement. Being part of a group in the process of personal exploration and discovery was exhilarating. It activated my whole being, like a kaleidoscope in which an existing pattern is thrown into dust and then, when the dust resettles, a brilliant new pattern emerges. Our trainers were highly skilled and appeared to be magicians who could draw out each individual's deepest soul themes and then weave the threads into a fabulous group tapestry, which in turn was part of a bigger collective web of meaning. A conversation would start over here and end up over there and we never knew where we were going or how we got there. I took part in gestalt therapy trainings and community for ten years and continued to teach it for many more years after that. The basic underlying theory focuses on the ways we interrupt our contact with experience and how we can use the practices of presence, awareness, deep listening, the imagination and experimental action, to re-connect and co-operate in the unfolding of the creative process. These skills and understandings have stayed with me ever since and become the bedrock of the groupwork skills and personal practices I use today.

Even this experiential groupwork didn't penetrate deep enough to free me, and the millions of others who were now part of a mass movement of change and transformation, from the limitations of the conditioned mind in which we were trapped. So, in the early '90's I joined the growing body of people practicing meditation and applying spiritual teachings to tame the ego, calm the mind and connect with authentic inner wisdom. As my spiritual practice did its work I fell deeper in love with writing and the inner world and I was compelled to escape from the city crowds into the creative freedom and solitude I found by living in the mountains and next to the sea. I sought out sanctuaries in beautiful places, hiding places from the injustices of the world, little islands of coherence in a sea of chaos. This took me out onto the fertile edges of social "normality" as a nomadic edge-dwelling pioneer and led into a strong motivation to heal the world, a huge mission in the face of which I have felt inadequate but which grows my skills, motivation and courage.

Before I complete this second chapter let's return to the story of me and my father and how his rage and my shame affected the development of my autonomy.

> Well into my thirties I unconsciously strove to win the approval I needed from my father by working hard and achieving in the world. By this time I had created my own business and was working freelance. One day I landed an

excellent job but on the way home after the interview I dissolved into tears. I had achieved exactly what I wanted yet I still felt empty. I realized the job was merely a symbol of what I really hungered for. I needed my father to say "I love you" not for anything I'd done or achieved, but simply for being me. No amount of achievement in the world was ever going to fill that hole. The success I needed was of another kind entirely.

Autonomy is a dynamic state of inner balance from which our unique potential flowers. My loving nature, the "inner Feminine," had become split from my will, the "inner Masculine." When the inner Masculine and the inner Feminine are wounded or in disharmony, there can be no wholeness or autonomy. Without a well-functioning will, which can hold healthy boundaries and focus on a consciously chosen purpose, there can be no healthy love. My father's punishing ways became internalised as part of my inner Masculine. This critical and controlling tyrant inside my head made me ashamed of my being and separated my will from my loving nature. Male and female were at war within me.

When a woman is in rebellion or reaction against her father's authority, she inevitably rebels against her own authority too. She can't discern what is good and healthy, nor feel safe in speaking and living her own truth, and she constantly sabotages herself. She may rebel against her true needs through addictions, eating disorders, toxic relationships and compulsive independence. However successful she is in the world, deep down she feels essentially unlovable and powerless, and she lacks the will to take actions that can make a real difference to her life. She may set out into the world with a goal or intention and then undermine herself. Or she may over-assert her authority and become strident, rigidly opinionated, brittle and controlling.

It's a familiar story. According to patriarchal religion, God is a harsh male judge and woman the fallen temptress, Eve. This myth lies deep within the western psyche. There are legions of rebellious daughters of the patriarchy in the world, wounded little girls hidden inside strong, independent women who cannot allow anyone to come too close. And there are legions of rebellious sons of the patriarchy too, unloved little boys hidden inside men who are either fearful of intimacy or dependent on it. When wounded women and wounded men get together, conscious loving is the challenge we are called to embrace, and this can be a long road.

I am beginning to understand it is not someone outside myself for whom I am longing and searching. Maybe, at some time, there will be someone to be my close friend and companion. But that will be icing on the cake. What I am truly longing for is a sense of completion, wholeness and harmony within myself. I need to experience the union of the healed Feminine: love, and the healed Masculine: will, within my own body, mind and soul.

When soul and Beloved are in each other's arms, it is easy to live simply, to shed image, possessions, imagined security and toxic habits. Then I no longer need anything to fill me up. The feeling of inner wholeness is so wonderful I require nothing else.

So, walking along the bush track today, where the light fell in shafts through the trees, I accepted the psychological legacy I inherited from my family as an important part of my destiny. This is what I have to work with in this lifetime, and it's the foundation for my growth. Some say when a soul reincarnates it chooses parents and particular circumstances to enable it to heal its unhealed parts. My task is to take the experiences I've had in my family and turn suffering into compassion. When I identify with my personality I recognise the pain, suffering, dramas and lost opportunities caused by this legacy. When I identify with the bigger picture of Soul, I experience gratitude and forgiveness.

Unconsciously I have believed myself to be a daughter of Eve, a woman fallen from grace. But this belief no longer fits. I know now I am a complex mix of love, light and shadow. This revelation lifts me in a moment from the drama of victim and persecutor to the responsibility of the autonomous adult. If I chose my father, I have also chosen all the other characters that have played on the stage of my life; and they have chosen me! All the pain I have experienced with people in outer reality has not been an expression of my unworthiness but a mirroring of the unhealed aspects of my soul; each conflict an opportunity to release myself from the karmic knots that bind me. The soul is a powerful attractor and the people who have challenged me most have been my best teachers. Synchronicity; the crossing of paths, is not chance but soul choice.

Here is a major piece of karma ready to be completed. I've written a letter to my father saying I'm ready to resolve and end our years of struggle, asking if he is open to doing that. I've sent it off with no expectation of outcome, knowing I have taken responsibility and done what I have to do to free myself for the next chapter of my life. My attitude towards this first man in my life has already become more compassionate, non-blaming and non-desiring. I have broken the spell that kept me bound to him in fear. I no longer need his approval; for having spoken my own truth to him, I now approve of myself. [10]

Soul Chapter Three: Mid-Life, the Spiritual Quest and the Process of Transformation

Authenticity is really about finding our connection with the rest of humanity, with nature and with cosmos, through being aligned with our highest truth.

You may be resonating with various parts of my story. I've been privileged to work closely with many people throughout my life and I know there is no such thing as a unique life theme. Our experiences are unique but the underlying themes are shared aspects of our humanity. By listening to each other's stories we discover our shared human story, a story embedded in place, culture and history. In the throes of the intense feelings that are part of the conscious healing process, I often lose sight of the bigger global perspectives of history and Soul, and I can take my suffering very personally. This is understandable and it is important to really feel that emotional intensity rather than to rationalise it away. But if we only see our stories as personal we prolong our isolation and risk getting stuck in shame and blame. Always remember the bigger perspective. The capacity to be present with whatever is arising, to experience it fully *and*, at the same time to remember our collective experience and the journey of the soul, is a crucial skill of conscious healing which we can develop.

But on with my story. Around the age of 40, I became disillusioned with nearly every aspect of my life and an irresistible pull from the inner world drew me into my spiritual quest. Searching for the lost pieces of my soul, I set off for wild, beautiful, expansive landscapes, first to the North-West Highlands of Scotland, and then to New Zealand. Whereas soul chapter two had been about action, experimentation, relationship, accumulation, building, and being "out there", chapter three was about being "in here" by learning to sit, wait, surrender, let go and empty. This was a big challenge and the spiritual practices that came to support me took me to places therapy hadn't begun to touch. Meditation and spiritual practice were the tools for a thorough process of clearing and cleansing that echoed down the soul line. While still half asleep to what I had chosen, yet irresistibly drawn forward and committed, I dedicated myself to this task of following my soul as I gathered tools for transformation and conscious evolution.

The more I emptied out limiting and painful old patterns, the more I became a channel for creativity. In chapter two, at the age of 34, I'd given up an interesting, well paid, full-time job to become a poet. I exchanged the challenge of travelling around Scotland supporting adult education tutors for the creative freedom of the visionary imagination, and then, realising poetry wasn't going to pay the mortgage, I'd gone on to create my own business. Now, age 44, I made two conscious decisions: to follow my creative process wherever it might lead me and to learn how to love consciously. These decisions weren't ideas I dreamed up but arose spontaneously from the depths of me. As a result I let go of many worldly privileges and possessions – my home, business, therapy practice, professional community, my income, partner and even my homeland. Chapter three had begun!

This letting go and emptying process continued in the beauty of New Zealand where I was intensely creative. I wrote books, explored my own approach to the new holistic discipline of transformational learning and conducted numerous learning experiments with groups. My life was no longer well rounded but had become eccentric. Although I had friends and community, I lived many of those years alone, exchanging intimate relationship with others for the self-intimacy of solitude and a growing relationship with my rich inner life. Sometimes loneliness gnawed at my vitals but I sent it away. I connected with a rich network of people on a similar path, and found soul friends, one of whom was Woods. Although our friendship was never a happy-ever-after partnership, and didn't tick any of the conventional boxes, he was the person who saw me most clearly, knew me most fully, loved me unconditionally and rejoiced in my creativity. He was a fellow explorer into the deep. His death, when I was 66, left me bereft and with the task of finding within myself the support he had given me.

This extract from a conversation I had with Woods for my book, *Living Your Passion, How Love-in-action is Seeding a Whole New World*, in 2007, says a lot about this third chapter of my life when spiritual practice and writing were my priorities and vehicles for transformation.

Living Your Passion

Woods: Are you saying that for you living your passion is somehow tied up with following your own creative path and rhythms?

Rose: That's right. At a certain point in my life I made a decision to follow my creative process wherever it might lead me. I've always come back to writing at times when I've made the greatest leaps of transformation. Writing seems to be at the core of living my passion. It's a wonderful tool for exploring experience more deeply and I love the challenge of bringing something into form, especially something as complex as a book. One of the key skills of writing seems to me to be the ability to listen deeply and to be receptive to what I "hear" or intuit. In the past, I've understood this as listening to my soul, a deeper, more expanded part of me than everyday consciousness. Now, I'm more interested in the idea that what is being heard or intuited is universal intelligence or spirit, and that we are all part of some vast, interconnected field of consciousness. I think projects which are successful arise from a field of collective consciousness and it's possible to "tune in" at some level to what is emerging. Maybe, in more profound moments, writing is a meeting between universal intelligence or "spirit" and the unique unfolding of individuality or "soul", and that's why it's so fascinating and compelling. For me, writing has been, and is, one of the most satisfying experiences of life, and it's certainly very closely tied up with the development of an authentic path and an authentic voice; and with the process of integration, which is essential for spiritual development.

However, writing hasn't always come easily to me. I've had to work at it over many years. When inspiration's flowing, it can be very exciting. There's a feeling of being carried by the creative energy, and if you follow, it leads you into the unknown, into new territory. But a lot of the time, it requires plain hard work and gritty determination. Once you've received the inspiration, you have to find the best form to express it and that involves a different set of skills and much pruning and editing. If you're writing for a particular audience, you have to consider what might be the best way to communicate with them, to reach and touch them. It's complex, and there's always more to learn. At some level, there's always a feeling of futility in the venture of trying to find words for subjective and mysterious experiences, which really can't be captured in words; or, in this case, trying to express leading edge ideas which are emerging very fast into the collective consciousness. It's a humbling experience coming up against the limitations of words and ideas and forms, and yet being compelled to continue the attempt.

There's a sacrificial aspect to following one's passion too. The creative process is about bringing everything to essence, or as close to essence as one can get, so anything which is not essential has to be let go. This leads to greater simplicity. It may be the simplicity of living with fewer possessions or less external "security". It can also be a simplicity which comes through a process of integrating what can be quite complex ideas or experiences into more inclusive wholes. So there's an emergence of greater complexity expressed as simplicity or wholeness. I have a favourite quote from the philosopher Martin Buber. In his seminal book, I and Thou, published in 1923, he talked about the challenge of finding the intrinsic form of a work and said, "It breaks, or it breaks me". There's a sense of being pushed to one's limits by a greater power and having to learn both the laws and the discipline of how to co-create with that. Part of the discipline is being willing to go beyond the "little me", the needs of the personality, self-indulgences and attachments. It's a process of holding a very clear focus and surrendering at the same time. You have to care enough to be willing to put in considerable time and energy, and yet be unattached to outcomes and not take it all too personally. It's really an exercise in aligning the personality with the soul's purpose, and the soul has very different values and priorities. Quite tricky! In this sense I think living one's passion is about being a creative artist, whether the work of "art" is one's own life, a community project, or in this case, writing a book.

Much of my life since that first leap has been a balancing act between this compelling call of the inner life and the necessity to participate in society; between writing as a tool of self-exploration and writing as an educational medium. The inner work always feeds and supports the outer work, and vice versa.

The Soul Journey

Woods: Before your migration to Aotearoa – New Zealand were there other radical shifts for you?

Rose: The second leap I took in '91-'93, when I made the conscious decision to follow my creative process. It took me first to the North West Highlands of Scotland and then to New Zealand on a soul journey adventure, which is ongoing. I discovered that following my passion, or my creative process, means allowing my unique path to unfold and being willing to go with that, even when it seems totally irrational or doesn't make any sense in terms of material security. That's the inspirational phase of the process: you can flow with it as an inner journey from the safety of home and you can also follow it as a physical life adventure. This can feel very risky at times, whether the risk is leaving physical comfort behind, or dropping a belief system and finding oneself in the unknown. I've had to learn how to support myself through the fear. Moving through fear and becoming aware of resistances are probably at the heart of most consciousness practices.

I came to Aotearoa, intending to stay for a few months then return to Scotland to participate in a new business, but like many others, I fell in love with New Zealand, and the South Island in particular, and that was that! After a few adventures I settled in Nelson at the top of the South Island and was offered a job teaching counselling theory and practice which was perfect for me at the time. The job enabled me to consolidate my psychotherapeutic experience, extend my teaching skills and make a contribution to the community. It supported me to get residency in New Zealand as well, and later a friend came along and helped me to buy a house, so I became quite settled for a few years. For me!

Woods: Oh, I bet you leapt again before long.

Rose: Yep! My third leap was in 2004, when I left my teaching job. I loved teaching but I was experiencing a growing tension between my own values and the desire to express myself authentically, and the values of the profession and institution I was working within, which felt more restrictive and rule-bound each time the institution restructured in response to the economic squeeze. I also had a strong feeling there was something more for me to do. I was still nurturing the vision I'd received when I first arrived in New Zealand, to create a Transformational Learning Community, and I wanted to give myself the time and space to see if this was indeed to be my soul work. So I went to live in the beautiful and remote community of Golden Bay until a clear direction emerged.

Beyond the Story-of-me

Woods: As you're telling your story, I'm thinking what an important vehicle personal storytelling is, both for integrating experience and moving beyond "the story-of-me".

Rose: Absolutely! Storytelling is such a powerful tool in many ways. Many people in my book, *Living Your Passion*, talk about the uncompromising nature of living one's passion, and it has felt like that for me too. Ultimately my highest value is to be free to explore and express my own experience and to understand what it really means to be a human being living at this moment in history. I've been freer than many people to do this as I have not had the responsibility of raising children to consider. Paradoxically, I've found the deeper I go into myself, the more I discover everyone else. I think 10% of the self is our uniqueness and 90% is our common humanity. The more I really explore my experience and understand myself, the more I find my belonging with the rest of humanity. Then I have more compassion for the human condition and I accept and love myself in a healthy and empowering way too. In this way, I've learned there is no separation between what truly serves me and what serves the whole.

Woods: Sounds like an important realization: when we actualize ourselves, we make our most important contribution to humanity.

Rose: Yes, I think the challenge and the opportunity at this time, when so many social institutions are being deconstructed, or have become corrupted, is for each individual to find their own authentic truth. There's an increasing pressure to do that, and my sense is the pressure comes from the evolutionary impulse itself. Authenticity is really about finding our connection with the rest of humanity, with nature and with cosmos, through being aligned with our highest truth and our authentic power. In order to make the evolutionary leap, which I believe is possible for humanity at this time, we first have to experience our connectedness fully. The beauty of it is, the more truly we express ourselves, the more we connect. As soon as we realize we are essentially interconnected with every other being, we don't have any other choice but to serve that interconnection. It becomes apparent we are not separate, and whatever we do, to or for another being, for good or ill, we also do, to or for our self. Ultimately there is only one Self, one consciousness. I'm moving from an intuitive understanding of this awesome truth, towards the experience of living it in every moment.

My retreat time in Golden Bay enabled me to do a lot of healing around that sense of separation from self, others and nature, and this is an ongoing process. Being in a very beautiful natural environment really helped me. I believe it is exactly this healing from separation to which the evolutionary impulse is calling us. Whenever any one of us heals in this way, we contribute to raising the collective consciousness to a level which will support the survival of our species and life on the planet.

From a conversation between Rose Diamond and Woods Elliott: *Soul work, the creative process in action*, from *Living Your Passion, How Love-in-action is Seeding A Whole New World.*[11]

There was another development in the story with my father during Soul Chapter Three. I wouldn't like you to think I abandoned my parents and flew off to the far side of the world without a care. I made many attempts at reconciliation, all to no avail. From my thirties onwards my father treated me with disdain. When I called he would pick up the phone and refuse to speak to me, handing me over to Mum with a grunt. And when I visited, even when I was sitting in the same room, he chose to ignore me. Imagine my surprise when, at my mother's funeral, he asked me to return to the UK to look after him. At that time I was loving my life in New Zealand, I had my own home, a job that suited me, a new relationship, friends and community. The last thing I wanted to do was to go back to England and take care of my Dad! At first I was furious, seeing his request as coming from the old-fashioned idea that it is a single woman's duty to look after her parents. But then, after considering further, I said yes. I remembered how spiritual teacher Ram Dass had defined his choice to take care of his aging father as a spiritual practice, and later used the limitations of his stroke in the same way.[12] I was inspired by how life's most challenging events can become opportunities to evolve consciousness and I thought, if Ram Dass can do it, so can I. I'm sure there was also still a longing in me to be loved by my dad. And so I said yes to him. My friends in New Zealand thought I was nuts. But by that time I was living according to my soul's agenda and not the preferences of my personality. And, for my soul, the most important thing was healing myself and doing whatever I could to heal my family.

I was with my father for nine months and then, seven years later, for another six months. As I've already told you, it was one of my most challenging missions but it did have some sweet moments. As he said, "we put some memories in the memory bank" and I learned a lot about my dad, myself and my family. The biggest shift for me was that I stopped being afraid of him. He no longer possessed the aggressive, dominating energy he'd had as a younger man and it was easier for me to experience my own power and to release some of the anger I'd been carrying for a lifetime. That enabled the healing process to move on. As I became more familiar with his life story I felt into what it might have been like for him to have grown up in poverty, sharing a bed with his three sisters in a small, dark tenement. And how it must have been for him when his father returned from the First World War, shell shocked and broken, and then went to dig clay from the slurries at the back of the house. Dad lived through the Second World War as a young man, with bombs exploding all around him in the darkness, as he walked home from a date with my Mum. He grew into manhood in an era when there was no conversation about everyday psychology or gender dynamics. As I entered into his life with imagination and empathy, I could feel how he might at times have felt painfully alone and stifled by the conditions of his life and how he may have defended himself against this pain by escaping into an ideal world, with dreams of "the beautiful people", with whom he could never live. During my stay with him I arrived at an understanding that, although he was a highly intelligent man, he didn't have the knowledge, awareness or skills to free himself from patterns of behaviour that kept him lonely and isolated. Finally I was able to see that he longed to connect with others but he simply didn't know how. He was trapped within his conditions of limitation. With this understanding I was able to stop taking his abusive behaviours so personally. This doesn't mean I condoned his aggression. I remembered his unpredictable temper and his need to control and how this badly affected me, my brother and my mother. But with understanding I could expand into a bigger cultural and historical perspective and see how we have all been moulded by the circumstances of our times. This empowered me to free myself from being a victim of abuse, to release the energy that had been locked up in fear and put it to work for positive change.

Nevertheless, at the end of my long visit I felt I had failed to love my father in the way I would have liked. Being true to my decision to return to my own life meant leaving him to survive alone and this hurt my heart as much as it liberated me. It was only after my brother's death fourteen years later that I was able to find the full forgiveness that finally freed me from the limitations of that relationship. Sadly, David never found forgiveness and died without resolution.

When I talk about forgiveness I mean the conscious releasing of anything that is interrupting and stifling the flow of love and creative energy. For me, forgiveness comes when I understand the conditions that have created a particular pattern of behaviour in myself or in another. This requires deep reflection and contemplation, sometimes over many years, and a willingness to look beyond what I previously thought was true. Forgiveness is difficult when we have been abused, traumatised or wounded by another and when we have held on tenaciously to judgments over a lifetime.

My decision to return to England to be with my brother in 2015 was also a continuation of my soul's desire to heal the family and be healed.

Soul Chapter Four: Eldership and Being of Service to the Whole

It is grief that expresses our human-ness more than any other experience. Only the human part of us dies. Spirit is eternal. Only the human in us experiences loss and separation. Spirit knows no separation. The most vital work of the human project and the grand design of Soul is to bring the eternal spirit of wholeness and interconnectedness into our daily human lives and to embody it.

During my first year in New Zealand I met two elders whose words of wisdom had a lasting impact on me. Barry Brailsford is a historian, archaeologist and author. I arrived shortly after he published his beautiful book, *"Song of Waitaha"*,[13] in which he wrote about three races of people: the black, the brown, and the white people, who migrated to Aotearoa in their waka (canoes) and lived together for one thousand years, building a nation founded on the ways of peace. This touched a deep longing in me to take my place among the One-Hearted People of Peace. My arrival at the top of the South Island of New Zealand felt like a homecoming and I decided to settle there.

The second elder who influenced me is Dr Rangimarae Turuku Rose Pere, Maori spiritual teacher and leader. She spoke of Aotearoa as a retreat centre for the world, a place where people "come to find the lost pieces of their soul". She cautioned, once we have found our lost pieces, we must go back to our homeland and take our wisdom with us to help heal the world. I always remembered this and, on that New Year's Day in 2015, when I decided to return to the UK to support my brother, her words were ringing in my ears. Both of these teachers inspired me to recognise and respect the wisdom of elders and to know that each one of us can make a lasting difference to other people's lives when we find our own truth and share it.

For me, this life chapter I'm calling Eldership is about completion, integration, coming to peace with life and being of service to the greater Whole. In my first two soul chapters I was preoccupied with discovering who I am in relation to the society and culture in which I live. My third soul chapter was dedicated to remembering who I am as a spiritual being. And now, in my fourth soul chapter I am returning to an interest in what it means to be a human being. Only now, I have the understanding and awareness that I am a spiritual being having a human experience. The more consciously I can live this human experience the better I bring together the human and the spiritual within me and embody my soul. As T.S. Eliot said:

> "We shall not cease from exploration
> And the end of all our exploring
> Will be to arrive where we started
> And know the place for the first time."

T.S. Eliot, Little Gidding, from Four Quartets[14]

Practising Compassion

My transition to becoming an elder began a year after I returned to the UK and came to settle in a beautiful part of North Wales, looking out onto the Snowdonia Mountains and across Cardigan Bay. As soon as I set foot on the land a ripple of recognition ran up from my feet, through my legs and into my heart, and I knew I was home. I first came here for three months to stay in a friend's cabin soon after Woods died. I needed to be somewhere quiet and close to nature so that I could write my way through grief. Every day I had nothing else to do but to get out of bed, walk across the room and sit down at the little writing table beneath the window, looking out onto the green and wintry, dishevelled garden. It was a time of beautiful simplicity when my daily writing practice grounded and supported me. While writing my book, *Portrait of a Gentle Man*, about Woods and his process of soulful living and conscious dying, I became very still and receptive, listening deeply. There's a certain point at which knowledge drops down from the head into the heart and becomes soul knowing, or gnosis. Here is a description of one such moment:

> What strikes me now is the sense of synchronicity and divine timing which reminds me I am held and guided by a bigger intelligence. Through Woods' dying, I received the absolute knowing that death is not to be feared,

everything happens at the right time and everything is as it is meant to be. This revelation instantaneously released me from any sense that my life has been less than perfect, even though it has often felt that way. In other words, it was an instantaneous and complete act of refocusing, acceptance and forgiveness. I was seeing from a higher and more comprehensive perspective than ordinary everyday consciousness – from the top of the mountain rather than from the valley floor. What I saw in that moment was that everyone in my life, including me, had acted in the only way we could in every moment, and if an action caused harm it was coming from unconsciousness or ignorance. Accepting that unconscious and ignorant behaviours are shared aspects of the human condition leads to compassion and self-compassion, rather than to hatred, enmity and self-loathing. It is only from a place of compassion that we can raise and transform consciousness. This is the only way we can re-write the past.

Perhaps this sounds simplistic or fanciful to your ears. I certainly don't mean to imply that we humans don't have any agency or choice or that violent actions are acceptable. We are not passive recipients of fate. We always have the choice to respond to life events consciously. When others act towards us in ways that cause us harm we can choose to draw boundaries, protest, make clear how we are affected and what we want, or to walk away and continue to live as lovingly as we can. To argue with what has already happened, or with what is happening that is beyond our control, is futile and keeps us contracted and stuck.

When it comes to the soul, "knowing" is not something arrived at by reading books – books can carry information and transmit the resonance of truth but *soul knowing*, or gnosis, is a visceral, whole person response. When we *know* we have connected with some truth that was already present within us but hidden from view and now has been revealed. It is, as Woods so often said, "a process of revelation".

During those days when Woods lay dying in Williamsburg, Virginia, I was in England with Maggie, someone who is not only friendly with death but passionate about it. The veils between the dimensions of earthly life and the afterlife thinned and I was able to move into a much bigger spaciousness of soul and a much deeper acceptance of life and death. My consciousness expanded and, although it is impossible now to capture this epiphany in words, I am changed. My best friend had died and yet in some essential way there was nothing missing. He left his body and I moved more securely into mine. A missing piece of the mystery was returned to me.

I believe this is what is meant by a Kairos moment: "a coming into being of a new state of things, … a moment of opportunity that escapes or transcends the passage of linear time… a moment of meeting in which a transcendent dimension (Kairos) intersects what is otherwise a one dimensional linear progression of time (Chronos). A time when "Two worlds came together and the soul returned (indwelling) to its rightful embodied place at the centre of emotional life."[15]

My understanding is that a Kairos moment marks an initiation into the next chapter of soul life. As part of my soul journey, my death walk with Woods completed the chapter that had begun 22 years before when I'd set the dual intentions to follow my creative process wherever it might lead me and to learn how to love consciously. These intentions would continue to be the focus of my consciousness practice as I moved further into the experience of wholeness. There is something mysterious and beautiful to me in this intuition that as Woods transitioned into his next chapter of soul life, beyond the Earth plane, he was a catalyst for me transitioning into my next chapter here on Earth in the body. Losing my best friend, rather than leaving me in loss, returned me to myself more fully than before.

We are all participants in an inter-connected and divinely orchestrated matrix of intelligence; an exquisite, synchronous whole within which we swim like fishes in the ocean, unaware of the medium in which we exist. We live in a multi-dimensional, holographic universe, held together by universal laws and sacred geometry and the soul exists simultaneously in many dimensions. Dear Woods, you have been a faithful companion on this journey. You dropped the outer housing, the natural intelligence of your physical body and your connection with Earth life, and walked through into another dimension of consciousness. Much as I miss you my dear friend, your death retuned and recalibrated my soul to a more expanded vibration. I am whole and home and so deeply thankful.[16]

Such illuminated insights may fade back into the bigger spaciousness from which they arise, and forgetfulness returns me to more limited perspectives, and yet I am forever changed.

At the end of my retreat, as I was leaving to return to my brother, I advertised in two local shops for a cottage to rent. A few weeks later I received a reply and I said yes to the cottage without seeing it; my landlord took me completely on trust too. It was effortless. When I arrived on a beautiful spring evening in April I was stunned by the beauty of the expansive view which spoke directly to my soul. This became my sanctuary for the next five years as my feet put down roots deep into the earth. Here, the restless reaching for something that had driven me my whole life, fell away. I felt freer than I've ever been yet I wanted very little for myself. Freedom seemed to exist, not so much in the ability to go somewhere, as in the willingness to stay and be here. I've had many experiences of being soul-led in my life but this is one of the clearest. Everything was arranged for me and I just had to walk through the doorway.

A few weeks later my brother died.

My Seven Years of Grief

Thus began what I've come to call "my seven years of grief" which carried me into the fourth chapter of Eldership. It is grief that expresses our humanness more than any other experience. Only the human part of us dies. Spirit is eternal. Only the human in us experiences loss and separation. Spirit knows no separation. The most vital work of the human project and the grand design of Soul is to bring the eternal spirit of wholeness and interconnectedness into our daily human lives and to embody it. This shift into a compassionate identification with all that it means to be human is essential for the future survival and thriving of our world. The seven years of grief which began after my brother's death was a rite of passage, a time when I was called to immerse myself fully in the experience of loss and grief and to face into the inevitability of death, not just for myself alone but as a way of contributing to the collective consciousness of humanity.

I wrote the first draft of *A Story of Transformation* soon after David died. It helped me to grow my understanding of the vital importance of the grieving process and led me to the creative work of developing *The Sitting with Death and Choosing Life Programme.*[17] The deepening intensity of our global problems a few years later, through the COVID pandemic, also marked a collective transition in which the necessity to face into our human shadow became urgent.

Until David's death I had been fairly satisfied with my progress in life. I had followed my dream, lived my passion, made my home in stunningly beautiful lands, quested for truth and authenticity, love and enlightenment, and listened for the voice of soul, obeying its guidance as best I could. Yet now, I realised while I had been driven hither and thither by the creative impulse, some essential parts of my being had been neglected. Touched by the loss of my brother, I took a trip down the lane of regrets and remorse and revisited the pain of wasted time, the times when I lacked courage, the times when love failed and the ways I compromised self-love. While I'd been pursuing the transcendence of creative excitement and spiritual freedom my mobility had become compromised by severe osteo-arthritis in both hips which prevented me from enjoying my lifelong love of walking and undermined the sense of independence I'd relied on since childhood.

The early demise of both Woods and David showed me, each in their different way, how neglecting the body's true needs and wisdom, can lead to premature death. This seems so obvious and yet I'd ignored this truth. Now, after years of neglect, my stiff body was calling out for love and nurturance and I could no longer turn away. A deepening into healthy self-love is an important part of the completion process of this chapter. After all how can I serve life if I don't first put my own house in order? How can I truly love if I don't love and honour myself? This certainly wasn't the first time I've faced these questions but my "seven years of grief" called me to face into my own shadow in a more radical, honest and uncompromising way than I'd ever done before and to find those aspects that were still unloved and unloving, so that I could transform the dull lead of unconsciousness into the golden light of wholeness.

It became clear to me that the osteo-arthritis that was compromising my ability to move forward with grace and ease was caused, at least in part, by the burden of unlived potential I'd been carrying for my family. When I say carrying, I mean I felt my family's pain acutely from early childhood, and absorbed their suffering into my blood and bones, so their suffering became my suffering. And then I carried this unprocessed pain into adulthood when I was compelled to come to an understanding of it and break free from it. I felt obliged to do all the living my parents and brother couldn't do and impelled to help others to liberate and empower themselves. These were impulses that rose through me so strongly there was no chance of saying no.

As I've told you, in order to fulfil my soul's mission - to heal myself and my family - I left home very early. I don't mean I left home physically but I clearly remember the day I began to separate from my family at seven years old and decided to spend as much times as possible away from them. Only now, when my damaged hips left me no choice but to stop running, was I able to appreciate the courage of that little girl who decided at seven years old to preserve her integrity by taking care of herself. Neither of my parents were mature enough to parent me in the way I needed as a child. They were unable to see me clearly apart from their own needs and shadows. They had come of age in a time of war and austerity and while they longed for me to live all they had not been able to live; they could also be envious and resentful of my freedoms and angry and punitive when I did not live up to their expectations or fulfil their dreams. The more they criticised me, the more I retreated from them and hid my true self. I fervently vowed to escape from them and find somewhere I could unfold into the fullness of authenticity. That unfolding has been a lifetime's work, requiring a lot of solitude.

I became a psychological orphan and it was that sense of being neglected orphans that David and I shared into our older age. I'd found the fierce determination and independence necessary to leave home so that I could discover myself and live my mission and yet there was loss for both of us in living without the support of a loving family. I learned a lot by reflecting on how that loss shaped my brother, and now I am beginning to fully appreciate and feel how it has shaped me. I was so identified with being a courageous spiritual warrior I didn't stop to consider the price of the experience. The hips are said to be part of the body where the unprocessed emotions of trauma and shame are stored. While David carried his burden on his stomach where it pressed on his heart, I carried mine in my hips. I inherited this tendency from my mother and from my grandmother before her.

It is no wonder so many healers burn out energetically when we are carrying so many burdens in our hearts and in our bodies. As I continued my personal journey through grief I was surprised to discover how deeply my brother's death affected me and how long the grieving process lasted. He was my last family member and my grief extended to include others in my family and then reached further back into ancestral roots in my quest to find understanding and compassion. I was supported in this work by my peaceful sanctuary in a beautiful part of Wales and some money my brother left me gave me all the time I needed to grieve fully. From the outside it might have appeared I was "sitting doing nothing" but, through the months and years of sitting with death, I came to appreciate the redemptive power within grief and how it furthers the collective healing journey.

In the spring of 2020, we went into lockdown for the COVID pandemic. Living as I do in this this sheltered part of the country, lockdown was a return to childhood innocence. I remembered what it is like to live without noise and air pollution, with very few cars on the road, the streets quiet and empty, nature coming back into its own dominion, all the lanes and meadows abundant with wildflowers. I was very aware of living within contrasting realities simultaneously; in my little piece of heaven, between the mountains of Snowdonia and the waters of Cardigan Bay, there was peace and sunshine; in the wider world the pandemic was raging and people were dying and afraid. We were all suddenly stripped of our civil liberties, including the right to reach out and touch a dying family member or friend. To the shock of grief was added the fear and erosion of identity that accompanies isolation. In my mind, the pandemic became linked with other existential threats of the climate emergency, the devastation of nature, the plundering of resources, the mass extinction of species with whom we share the planet and increasing intolerance and violence between humans. Many people deeply mistrusted the motives behind the vaccination programme and the loss of our ability to discern the truth gave rise to polarisation and fragmentation among previously like-minded people and a growing cynicism in relation to our leaders and politicians.

In the midst of existential crisis, a quiet power tapped me on the shoulder and asked me if I was willing to take up the task of spreading grief awareness. I knew this project had my name on it and I said YES. From that moment I was committed to the evolution of the *Sitting with Death and Choosing Life Programme* and I took up the mission to educate, encourage, empower and equip people to move through grief towards fulfilling participation in community life. There could not have been a better time to launch such a programme.

Only now, as I'm emerging from my seven years of grief am I beginning to understand this as a transition into eldership. Just as the earlier mid-life transition in my early forties led me through a dark night of the soul and the letting go of an old identity, so has this. I can see now that mixed up with all the grief of loss there was suffering caused by my resistance to the transition. I was attached to my old identity as a spiritual warrior and I didn't want to let it go. I treasured my life of solitude and fought against the constraints of living in relationship. Even though my lifestyle provided all the peace I needed to complete my soul work, I judged it and found it wanting. I didn't want to exchange my restless spirit of adventure for the stillness and embodied presence I now enjoyed. And I certainly resented growing old. The completion of this book has taken its own time and it is in the patient weaving and re-weaving of the threads of my lifetime that I have finally found peace, fulfilment and deep gratitude. Here is a poem I wrote while I was recovering from my second hip surgery which finally set me free to walk again in a new way.

Re-membering all the lost worlds

I am reading a book about becoming a woman poet
and re-visiting Adrienne Rich.

Here, now, the radical light of early spring is softened by a thin veil of cloud,
downstairs, news from the war in Ukraine.

Cushioned in bed by downy covers, I have no reason to complain
and yet I complain riotously, out of favour with my bones,
at odds with being human, I don't belong in my body
as I scribble words in a hand I can barely decipher.

I remember standing at a bus stop, many years ago,
there on the dirty city pavement, a troubled young woman
clutching a brand-new copy of "A Wild Patience Has Taken Me This Far",
I can smell the virgin pages now.

I boarded the bus and came home
to the companionship of this woman's mind,
a restless, challenging mind that would not settle,
always seeking for the whole truth, yet always compromised
by the approximation of words that is the poet's craft.

I gave myself to writing poetry with passion,
racing home from work to sit and listen
to the whispers of the empty page.
Alone there at the coal face, digging for diamonds in the dust,

not knowing where I was going, or why, but intent and intense,
driven toward some old promise I had made and forgotten
and which now, will not let me go.

What did she want, that troubled young woman?
Pushing her way through the unconscious earthiness
of existence, through tears and loneliness,
to open doors and windows in her mind
and gaze up at the stars so many light years away.

Where did the mind of that young woman, in 80's Britain,
meet and mingle with the mind of a brilliant American poet,
alive on a different continent? And where
does this mind intersect with ancestral voices, voices locked in coal,
under the earth, where trees are turned to blackened ancient sunlight?

And what is the task of a woman poet today
in a world at war with life?

Passion is not rational and yet it longs
for form, containment, the tussle of intense, full-on relationship.
Today, perhaps, what feels like sickness and the falling away of life,
is the release of a protective husk that has had its day.
And what remains, deep within the mind, within remembrance and the
earth,
is the uncontrollable energy of life, seeking expression,
longing to fulfil its destiny, in a new movement and configuration,
as a fountain of love.

In the face of war and insanity,
when power is distorted into wanton destruction,
I plant my stake as a woman poet,
here, now, today,
I claim my YES to life.

Rose Diamond, [18]

An Invitation to Complete Your Life Review

I have explored the life review in some detail, using my own experience for illustration, as a way to put personal grief into the context of conscious healing, soul work and the much bigger process of cultural awakening and transformation. Your life story is unique *and* you are part of a collective story of awakening consciousness. Your soul gives you your uniqueness – the particular bundle of skills, gifts, meaning, purpose, direction and sense of destiny that motivates and unfolds through you. The more you discover yourself as a soul the more you can fulfil your particular role in the bigger scheme of life and the more fulfilment you will experience. And, you are never separate from the currents of the bigger ocean in which we all move.

The shift into a compassionate identification with all that it means to be human is essential for the future survival and thriving of our world. Through our grief journeys we have the opportunity to develop essential skills for grieving well. As well as enabling the completion of a beloved relationship, grief can also be part of the transformational process and, sometimes, is necessary for the completion of a soul chapter. At the heart of the transformational process is the expansion of consciousness. Those of us on conscious healing journeys can become skilled in co-operating with this transformation of consciousness and may move into the next new stage of consciousness emerging now across the planet, which I call Whole Mind-Whole World.[19] Individually, our most challenging life experiences are fuel for our soul work. Collectively, we can use the chaos and mayhem of our global problems as fire for the evolution of consciousness and culture.

You and I are part of this evolution and a vital skill is the ability to identify the soul choices you have made. Some of these will have been operating in your life unconsciously, guiding you intuitively, throwing up synchronicities, magnetising opportunities and connecting you with all the people who have played important roles in your life drama. Your soul choices also show up in repeating patterns of behaviour that cause suffering for yourself and others. As you make these choices conscious your values will appear more brightly and your soul will guide you even more powerfully, you will connect more strongly with your own authentic meaning, purpose and direction. This will enable you to find peace with difficult life events, to embrace your gifts more fully, and to offer them more passionately.

The Practice of Life Review

Set aside an hour or two when you won't be interrupted and create a sanctuary space where you feel held and comfortable. You may need to break the review into several sessions so be aware of your energy and pace yourself.

This process will stir whatever in you is as yet incomplete and I recommend that you do it at a time when you are feeling resilient and well-resourced.

It can be difficult to see your own deeply conditioned patterns and choices. If you need support reach out to a coach or therapist with whom you already have a relationship or contact me and my team via my website.

Make a timeline and map the story of your life

+ Begin by making a timeline of your life, starting at birth and ending at your current age, or go further into the future if you wish.

+ Go through your life chronologically writing down anything you feel has played a significant part in shaping you. Include difficult memories that may still have an emotional charge, positive life events which revealed your true emerging self and synchronicities or times of high excitement that changed the course of your life. Mark these on your timeline, perhaps using different colours to differentiate between the challenging and the happy memories and put them on opposing sides of the line.

+ When you have finished you may have an intuitive sense of where your life chapters begin and end. Mark these on your timeline.

+ Now begin with your first soul chapter, Childhood, Family and the Cultural Thesis, and reflect on:

The physical and emotional environment that shaped you as a child, and how?

What was it about your parents, your school or any other major influences – other significant adults, siblings, the culture or country you grew up in, your church or religion – that supported you to feel free, whole, engaged with life, creative, safe to express yourself and loved?

And what made you feel unfree, fragmented, repressed, unsafe and unloved?

What beliefs, conscious or unconscious, did you absorb from this environment or adopt in rebellion against it? Write these down.

+ What creative adaptations did you make as the difficult aspects of your life emerged? For example, I used writing and the imagination to create my safe space as a child. And I found friends with loving families who took me in and nurtured me.

Have these creative adaptations continued to support you throughout your life?

Are there any ways they have limited your experience?

+ What soul choices did you make during these years?

How have they given you direction, purpose and meaning?
How have they stretched and challenged you?
What have you sacrificed in following these choices?
What have you learned and how have these choices developed your character?

◆   Identify any beliefs that were driving your behaviour.

Are there beliefs you need to let go now?
People you need to forgive or apologise to?

◆   Whether you believe in the soul's reincarnation or not, for now, play with the idea that you chose your parents and all your life circumstances. Can you see any ways that the people and circumstances that moulded your life gave you exactly what you've needed to become the unique individual you are today?

Does this change anything?

◆   End your reflections on your first life chapter by writing a list of all the ways you appreciate yourself. And all the people and circumstances you are grateful for from your first chapter.

Now take a rest, go out in nature, move your body, empty your mind, expand into spaciousness.

At another time, and when you are ready, move on to your second life chapter. You will find information about how to take your inquiry further, under next steps at the end of the book.

Identify Your Soul Choices, Key Values and Shadow Aspects in Each Soul Chapter

As you identify the soul choices you've made in each chapter you will become much clearer about what drives you, the natural strengths and gifts you have, and the shadow side of your gifts. This should help you enormously in understanding the past and current challenges in your life; to what extent you have honoured your soul contracts, and what you can do next.

For example, in my Soul Chapter One, I made these vital choices:

Soul Choice 1: Realising my parents were not able to take care of me in the ways that I needed to thrive, *I decided to preserve my integrity and autonomy by mobilising my own resources and taking care of myself as best I could.*

Soul Choice Two: *I vowed that I would sit out the captivity I was experiencing at home and at school and then set off to find the "something more" I knew was possible.*

These choices were made instinctively and informed my actions. They didn't become conscious until much later. When I look at them now I can make sense of my life in a whole new way and I can see myself more clearly, both as a soul and as a personality. I can see where my challenges have been in relationships and why events unfolded as they did.

From Soul Choice 1, I see that I came into this world with a ready-made package of self-reliance, resourcefulness, determination and strength. Later in life, these qualities supported me and drove my work in the world. The shadow side of this is what I call compulsive independence, a drive to be independent which is so strong it doesn't take account of the needs of relationship. I've shared some of the struggles I had in wresting my autonomy from the grip of my father which instigated this drive in me. I've had many relationships in my life – personal and professional, intimate and social, long lasting and ephemeral and, like most people, I've come up against my own repeating relationship patterns and training grounds. In the second half of life I've been learning a lot about my need for others and how to balance autonomy with closeness and to build trust by drawing clear boundaries. It's the balance between the inner Masculine and the inner Feminine which I've talked about before. There's a particularly unattractive shadow aspect which is to take the resources that seem to come so easily as a sign of entitlement and specialness and to exploit the generosity of others. I see this as a pattern which underlies much of the abusive behaviour that is destroying our world. There is in human nature a complex and deadly mix which combines feelings of neglect and "not-enoughness" with a strident determination to take care of oneself, and take what one needs, without recognising the needs of others. The courage to track down and clearly recognise our imbalances and blind spots, and to own them, is a vital part of the work of conscious healing in which we can liberate humanity by starting right here within *this* life, *this* self, this fractal of the greater whole, I call me.

I encourage you to use this example as a stimulus to conduct your own life review. As you identify your soul choices, key values and shadow aspects in each soul chapter, you will be strebgthened and liberated.

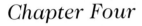

Chapter Four

Existential Crisis and Transpersonal Grief

Shock can be an Opening into the Transformational Process

We can choose to use every world-shaking event as an opportunity for personal transformation and hold an intention for a global transformation of consciousness.

I am sketching a map of sorts and a set of skills you can use to support you in co-operating with the naturally evolving healing process of life so that you can live a more fulfilling life:

First, having a reason why, or an uplifting philosophy will motivate you;

Secondly, being clear about your own values and soul choices will provide direction.

And third, setting an intention to bring yourself in line with your values and choices will create momentum.

Shock can provide a fertile ground for intention setting. At this time, when we are bombarded with news of shocking catastrophes and humanitarian crises, a common response is to shut down in the face of overwhelm and choose to be numb rather than to feel our sorrow and despair. But, if we remain awake and aware, we can set an intention, even when we are in shock, and this intention will support us to keep moving forward rather than getting stuck in the emotional impact of shock.

Shock is a disruptor. It shakes us awake and tears through the veils of everyday, habit-bound reality, for a while rendering us vulnerable, tender and humbled. When the shock of sudden loss and death breaks open the heart we may feel the power of love more strongly than usual. It's strange to say that most of us, most of the time, keep our love under wraps; we are afraid of the power of love and don't know what to do with it when it breaks free. As well, most of us have experiences of not loving as fully as we could and this realisation can hurt. After a death we have a short window of opportunity in which we can enter a more expanded, open state of consciousness. This window will fade. The momentum of habit is strong and has deep roots. Very soon these habits will sprout and weeds will quickly grow and cover the open window. If you want to stay expanded you need to be vigilant and plant a firm intention at this point.

When I received the news of my brother's death I wasn't jumping up and down with glee thinking, "Yippee, this is an opportunity for transformation." Shock is a difficult state and I was simply in it and living it and getting through it as best I could. I had to move through those first stages of shock, loss and grief before I could make the choice to heal myself and to evolve consciously. As I made that choice I brought my will into line with the deeper truth of Soul and I became an active participant in the process.

Let me give you some other examples of what I mean when I speak of the opportunity that can arise to plant an intention through the shock of a sudden death. Let's consider some of the sudden deaths we are experiencing globally. I'm sure you remember the bombing of the Twin Towers in September 2001, when our current apocalyptic chapter of human life began. The event sent shock waves throughout the world and was a gamechanger. Before 9/11 and after 9/11 we lived in different worlds. The recent COVID pandemic in 2020, is another example. In any global catastrophe such as these we have no choice in what happens but we do have a choice as to how we respond.

Walk the Edge Between Life and Death

The world was never the same after September 11th, 2001.

I was living in New Zealand and awoke to a spring day of clear clean sunlight which cut through my lethargy and stirred me into hope and excitement. I had stopped listening to the news, so I was oblivious to what had happened in New York a few hours before. I put on some music and danced a dance of thanksgiving and promise before hurrying off to work.

I was teaching that morning with my co-worker, Peter, and when I met him at the door of our office his face was ashen.

"Hey, what's up?" I asked.

"Haven't you heard?" he cried. And then he told me the story of the Twin Towers. Instantaneously the terror hit my solar plexus and travelled the length of my spine, as it was meant to, and I joined the shock wave sweeping the world. At some level of my being I had been waiting for this moment. An awareness of the knife-edge we humans walk between life and death, the light and the dark, had been with me since adolescence. Surely this was the signal for the end of the world as we had known it.

This flagrant act of violent aggression and contempt against the World Trade Centre, an icon of western privileged wealth, brought to the forefront of everyone's attention the grievances of the Islamic people that had been ignored for a very long time. The terrorist attacks flouted all the international rules and agreements for the conduct of war and threatened our western way of life, awakening ordinary citizens into a state of heightened anxiety. This terrorism recognized no boundaries, no territories, no rank, no conventions and no compassion. If the icon of the world economy in the most powerful country in the world could be annihilated, then anything was possible.

Shaken, Peter and I made our way to the classroom and found our students in a similar state of shock and grief. There was no question of following our lesson plan. We sat in a circle, placed a lighted candle in the middle and sat together in silence. Then, over the next few hours, we shared our feelings and responses to the catastrophe. We were more than a group of students and teachers with a common interest; we became a community joined at the heart.

For me, 9/11 held a revelation and pointed towards a heightened sense of purpose. I was emerging from a long winter's vigil in which I had been confronting some painful personal limitations which prevented me from connecting deeply and intimately with others. I felt trapped behind a thick, opaque membrane which kept me captive and lonely. The shock of the catastrophic explosion of the Twin Towers breached this membrane and at last I could reach out a hand and find another hand reaching for mine. Some ancient veil was gone.

That morning as we expressed our horror and compassion for the dead and dying and their loved ones, it brought home to us the fragility and impermanence of human life. We were reminded how it is possible to walk out the door in the morning and never come back, or to see a loved one off in the morning of a normal day and never see them again. If this is possible then every interaction counts. This moment now is the only one we have for letting our loved ones know we care and they matter. When we stare opened eyed into the inevitability of death there is no place for carelessness or meanness.[1]

9/11 brought me the knowing that world peace has to begin within me and with healing within my family. Three months later I was given the chance to bring this insight into my personal life. In December 2001, my mother died of a broken heart and with a worn-out body. Not long before her death she spoke to me about the mass burning of cows in open fields throughout the UK, following an outbreak of "mad cow disease". She loved animals and this carnage was too much to bear. Her death led to my decision to return from New Zealand to the UK for a year to take care of my father. I saw clearly how the shock of her death tore through his habitual walls leaving a gaping hole in his daily existence as he faced being alone for the first time in his life. This left him, for a short time, more open and vulnerable, and so I went to stay with him for a year to help him through his transition. This was one of my most challenging missions as my father was entrenched in a stage of consciousness that allowed little room for seeing another's perspective. I had always had a very difficult relationship with him, and this was one of the toughest actions I could take. Much of me was screaming NO! However, I could see how losing his wife of sixty years created an opening and, if there was ever a time when I could help him and heal the rift between us, the time was now. So, I said yes and, although it was extraordinarily difficult, I didn't regret my decision. The challenging relationship I had with Dad was the training ground in which I could begin to balance, at mid-life, my need for autonomy with my desire to love and care. The death of my mother left a space in which I could begin to explore my more feminine side and Dad was one of my greatest teachers. Even though I was a trained and experienced whole person therapist, with him I was always a complete beginner and I felt keenly the inadequacy of my skills. I left at the end of the year knowing I still had a lot to learn and with a sense that I had failed to love him and help him as I had wished. Nevertheless, it was a special time and what I learned about my father, my family and myself, were pearls of great price. I had to accept the tough lesson that, despite all my skills, I could not bring about the changes I longed to make in my relationship with my father. Even so it was worth trying. We never know the seeds we sow or how we affect another.

A big shock explodes the fragile reality we have constructed from a ragbag of physical, emotional and mental habits and can oust us from our comfort zone. Our habits of thinking and behaving hold us and provide a sense of security, and they also limit us. They include belief systems that filter the way we interpret reality and how we see ourselves and the world. When change happens unexpectedly – whether in the form of a death, an accident, a natural disaster, a betrayal in a relationship, or even falling in love - we are shaken to the core. Just like the gaping hole and collapsing walls of the Twin Towers, the way we've conceived reality can crumble in a moment leaving us as exposed and tender as a crab without a shell.

These dark times can be portals that lead to the greatest breakthroughs. If you can find a way to sustain yourself and you are well enough resourced inwardly to tolerate being in the unknown, change and disruption in the status quo can mark the beginning of a new level of growth and harmony. Eventually something new emerges - a new more expanded sense of self; a more immediate and easy access to the feelings of the heart, or a renewed sense of purpose and appetite for life.

Loss creates a gap which can be filled with new awareness, creative energy and inspiration. When our habitual defenses are breached, we feel more and we're more aware of our need for others. We're not just living on the surface of life and getting by; we're thrown into our own mysterious depths and existential questions. This is a time when we may be able to change some very old and deeply engrained habits; a time when Soul can nudge us into a bigger perspective.

When we resist making the necessary changes Soul's knock on the door will come around again, in another form, and more forcibly, until we sit up and take notice. But then, after a while, if we don't respond, the portal gradually closes, we pull another security blanket around us and go back to sleep. If we remain resistant and continue to ignore the call, eventually Soul recognizes there is no real desire for a soul-led life, and withdraws, awaiting another lifetime.

When the Earth Moves Take Your Stand

Here is another story of how loss can be a wake-up call and an opportunity for intention setting. In 2011, the house I was sharing with Maggie, which had been her home for ten years, was destroyed by flood and landslide. This short extract from my book, *Whole Mind-Whole World*, begins at the moment Maggie looked out of the window on an evening of torrential rain and saw the lawn moving, as the trees in the steep bank above us lost their grip in the earth, and the bank began to crumble.

"The strange thing was, as soon as we saw the earth moving across the lawn, we both recognized this as the wake-up call we had been waiting for. I had no idea it would come in this form but I had been expecting it for thirty years - a knock comes at the door, it's a civil emergency, you can only take one bag, and your life is never the same again. And here it was - an opportunity for realignment with Soul values…

The next afternoon I picked my way gingerly through the mud, back to the house, to collect some food. What had been our home was now a damp shell filled with the stench of dereliction. I emptied the contents of the fridge into a bag and threw in supplies from the pantry. Then I slung the heavy bag across my shoulder and trudged back over the boulders and potholes. In those moments I experienced a strong identification with all exiled people throughout the world. Images of refugees made homeless by war and natural disaster filled my heart's eye. I saw families forced to leave their villages, taking only what they could carry, heading into very uncertain and unknown futures. I was now one of them. Stripped of material wealth and possessions, with no home, no family and only a fistful of dollars to support me; this was my vulnerable reality.

And yet, in the very same moment as I experienced this loss and raw exposure, I also knew I am one of the most privileged people on Earth. Even in this now bedraggled paradise, I was part of a caring and compassionate community and blessed to be able to say, "I'll use this as an opportunity to evolve consciously…"

I held these two truths in my mind at once: the clear seeing of my fragile situation and the deep knowing that we would be taken care of and would thrive as a result of this seeming catastrophe…

On that first morning, and thereafter, Maggie and I were certainly shaken but we were very glad to be alive. Right from that first moment when the land slid, we had both known this was a potential liberation and an opening for radical change. We knew we were in this together for a reason and that it was an opportunity to put into practice everything we had been learning about impermanence and radical trust in the spiritual studies we were doing together. Even though the circumstances were frequently demanding and stressful, as long as we kept surrendering to what was happening in each moment and didn't resist, we were mostly able to maintain a positive state of mind. Whenever we gave way to fear and attempted to resist by thinking this was unfair and shouldn't be happening to us, suffering quickly followed. That in itself was a valuable lesson. In the aftermath, it was those who could see no meaning, and therefore felt victims of the flood, who suffered the most.

As we took the practical steps necessary to ensure our safety we were aware of being completely in the hands of life itself: a power much bigger than "me". We had lost our home and between us we had very little money so we had no idea how to solve our immediate practical problems. Yet everything unfolded effortlessly and we were perfectly taken care of. This was an opportunity to surrender the egoic mind with its attachment to "me" and "mine" and to realign with Whole Mind. This shift in consciousness moved us out of our old identities, which were still somewhat reactive, and into a completely new, responsive and co-creative relationship with life. From this expanded state, we knew intuitively, everything is interconnected and interdependent and we are all part of one life, one energy flow. It would take a few years after the event to integrate these realisations and to become more stable in this new consciousness but the crisis was the opening that enabled us to see and experience a new reality. The opportunities to choose kept coming."[2]

Our sudden shocking loss was a transformational opportunity. When I talk about transformation I am talking about the potential that lies within each one of us to lift our consciousness from a small-minded view focused on "me" and what I need and want, to a more expanded view which focuses on the needs of the whole and on how I can serve the greater whole by contributing my unique creative gifts and authentic expression. This expanded view includes "me" and my needs and develops alongside empathy, compassion, and a heart-felt love and dedication to life. In other words, our human and spiritual aspects become one integrated whole.

Five years after the flood, the wake-up call of my brother's sudden death was another opportunity to experience my next expansion of consciousness, soul work and service. At some level, through those trembling weeks, as my old identity was falling away, I knew this and it helped.

Bringing Death to the Table

"In the midst of these formidable challenges...we are being called to the next stage of evolutionary history. This new era requires a change of consciousness and values – an expansion of our worldviews and ethics. The evolutionary impulse moves us forward from viewing ourselves as isolated individuals and competing nation states to realizing our collective presence as a species with a common origin and a shared destiny."

Mary Evelyn Tucker and Brian Thomas Swimme[3]

At the beginning of lockdown I joined a group of practitioners from different parts of the UK to explore how we might spread community conversations about death, dying, grief and loss, as a support for individual wellbeing and also to stimulate a shift to a culture which is fully supportive and aligned with life. Fourteen weeks into lockdown, in July 2020, five of us met for an online conversation. We explored our personal experiences of the Coronavirus pandemic and the challenges and gifts we were finding in lockdown. The following summary shows how, each in our own way, we used the crisis as an opportunity to focus our values and intentions.

Alexandra Derwen[4] lives in Snowdonia in North Wales and has all her life been in service of the dying and the bereaved, quite naturally. In recent years she started to hold circles calling death and grief to be our teachers. Her work has grown rapidly all over UK, Ireland and Europe with invitations throughout the world. Preparing end of life doulas, ceremonialists and grief keepers for the task is, primarily for Alexandra, a community development endeavour. We are in the process, she feels, of creating a wholesome culture that can hold shadow and nuance so that death and grief can return from the margins back to their rightful place at the heart of community life.

Alexandra was in Spain, walking the Camino de Santiago as a pilgrimage and path of spiritual renewal, when the pandemic broke there. People were terrified and confused as angry police with guns moved them off the streets and into isolation. She had no choice but to leave Spain and, on arrival home in the UK, she self-isolated just in case. Four days later she fell ill and knew she had caught the virus. During self-isolation she realized she might die. She experienced the grief of that and then, coming out, she was in a deep meditative state in which her most important focus was to drop resistance and fear, and to trust. She sensed COVID to be a collective initiation bringing the needs of the dying into public awareness. And she saw it as an invitation to atone for all we have done to each other and to the planet.

(Note: In 2020 Alexandra experienced a shift in understanding about gender and made the move to using they/them pronouns as a non-binary person. Alexandra has given consent for the text to retain the "she" pronoun as that was indeed the case when we were in dialogue at the time.)

Anneé Bury has walked alongside grief and death for most of her life. At the time of the pandemic, age 66, she was passionate about exploring how we, as a culture, can heal our disconnection from death and bring death back into life. She saw the pandemic as a catalyst reconnecting us with our hearts, our emotions, and in particular our grief, and thereby our love for all that is life. Over her lifetime she has been a nurse caring for dying children and adults, a sociologist teaching about death in our culture, a hospice educator, a shamanic healer, a cancer and end of life mentor, a funeral celebrant and a ceremonialist. She cares passionately about all that is challenging and shadowy because she sees it is this dark underworld that holds humanity's hidden jewel. She almost died when she was born and has learnt to live fully following an aggressive cancer diagnosis in her fifties.

Until late January 2020, Anneé was in South Africa where she had been practicing reconciliation between humans and the Earth, with other species, between races and colours of skin. When she returned home to the UK, she fell ill the next day. She didn't think she had COVID but in any case had no fear of death, having already been through the challenge of living with cancer. In a shamanic process she communicated with the COVID19 virus and received the message that the virus itself is not malevolent but brings the lesson that humanity has to repent and there is no more time.

At the same time as welcoming COVID as an opportunity, she was also aware of the reality for so many people who were dying alone in hospital, or at home, separated from family; and the many others who were experiencing trauma and distress in the grief experience, as family members were not given the time and support to let go of their loved ones or the opportunity to provide them with a dignified death. Far from reconciliation, Annee saw the political and media discourse around COVID focusing on fear of dying and death and felt, in many ways, lockdown created more separation and personal shut down. Nevertheless, she saw COVID19 as a potential wake up call for humanity, finally bringing death to the table and raising the question, when are we going to take responsibility for what we have done to the planet?

Gloria Tinu Ogunbadejo[5] resides in Essex, London. She is an ordained minister, a mental health practitioner, a spiritual holistic counsellor, a Life and Funeral Celebrant, an Ancestral Healing Coach and Practitioner and a journalist. The focus of her work is in trauma, loss, bereavement and ancestral healing. Gloria first came face to face with the virus when her daughter, who was working in Europe, came home and fell very sick.

Then, through her work with Diabetes UK, Gloria witnessed much fear, suspicion, confusion and helplessness as people became ill. She likened the shock of the disease to a plague and saw how an event such as this can bring us together as one humanity or separate us yet further, showing the divisions between people more clearly and what needs to be healed. Peaceful moments within which nature was making itself known were followed by the next explosion of fear, panic and separation and Gloria saw the pandemic as a make or break time. When people are laid bare and opened up by facing death, there is an opportunity to take another path towards healing. Despite all the heartbreak, Gloria holds a space for hope.

Jos Hadfield[6] lives near Helston in Cornwall where she hosts Death Cafes, online and locally. She trained with the Vinyana association in Spain and is a teacher in Spiritual Companionship at end of life, offering workshops in this and in caring for carers. She also sings and is co-director of Liminal Choir, a small group of compassionate beings who sing at bedside. Jos was a long way from the centre of the crisis and she found huge solace in nature especially with the benevolence of the weather. She met many people out walking and connecting with nature, as if for the first time, and she saw this as a great gift. She found it surreal holding these two levels at once: the great peace she was experiencing and the widespread affliction of so many others elsewhere. Her daughter was expecting a first child and a distressing labour was made more complicated by the isolation of COVID, making it a bittersweet event.

Teaching Tai Chi and running Death Cafes on the internet, Jos was learning new ways of connecting all over the world and she recognized with relief that there was no need to get on a plane to do her work. Although it can be harder on the internet to express and be with strong emotions, through her Death Cafés she connected with the loneliness, anxiety, fear and loss of those who felt out on a limb and unsupported. Jos saw COVID as a major global wake-up call in which she held a space for joy.

For me, this was a time of experiencing the complexity and range of my emotions. After an initial period of alarm, like Jos, living in a remote area of outstanding natural beauty, in this pause between breaths, when humanity was brought to a standstill, I identified with Nature itself. For a short while CO_2 emissions declined, Nature was able to breathe and the land was at peace. I wondered what might change in human consciousness and behaviour if the same persistent media coverage given to the pandemic was also focused on the climate emergency? How many deaths from climate related catastrophes have there been today?

The pause in busy-ness as usual was an opportunity to step back and see how much more simply I could live and to recognize that the most important thing is to stay connected with life. While acknowledging a new level of responsibility for my own part in the consumer culture that is destroying the planet, I also realised that the changes I long for are unlikely to come in my lifetime and that conditions on the planet are likely to get worse. And yet, I believe, this is not a reason to give up but rather to extend our efforts as the seeds of consciousness we plant now will grow and eventually, when the time is right, life will prevail. In this spirit, I became intensely focused on my creative work, completing the *Sitting with the Death and Choosing Life* resources and offering a facilitator training.

In our group conversation in that summer of 2020, the five of us acknowledged the masses of people who don't have the time or opportunity to sit back and reflect and for whom the disruption caused by COVID felt like the end of the world. If we look to the global south, to India and parts of Africa for example, we see huge populations with very little food and other life-threatening conditions. COVID presaged the end of the world as we have known it, with the breakdown of systems and climate. And perhaps it was preparing us for the next wave, and the next, of turbulence, suffering and transformation. Within these extremes of human experience, those of us on a conscious healing path can inhabit an inner stillness and find places and people that support us to feel whole. Sometimes it is necessary to drop into a profound hopelessness and make a space for that. Amidst the wounding, the trauma, and the unrest, we may discover a deeper acceptance of the human condition and our responsibility for life on Earth.

By accessing joy and connecting at the heart, we nourish Soul and Planet and keep alive an awareness of what is possible. Amidst all the chaos, disaster, death and suffering, we can find the deep love and the true wealth we've been longing for.

This conversation first appeared in The Sitting with Death and Choosing Life Conversations Volume 4: Grieving for Our World[7]

Questions for Inquiry

Have you experienced shock as a wake-up call? If so, what happened and what did this bring into your awareness?

Since COVID19 and lockdown how have your life and your consciousness changed?

Reflect on the transformation unfolding in our world and imagine planting a stake of intention into the fertile soil of transformation. Is there an intention you'd like to plant today?

Going forward into the inevitable turbulence to come, how might you use your gifts to make a difference to people and planet?

Chapter Five

Sitting with Death

To go in the dark with a light is to know the light.
To know the dark, go dark. Go without sight,
and find that the dark, too, blooms and sings,
and is travelled by dark feet and dark wings.
Wendell Berry, To Know the Dark[1]

The loss of my dearest friend, followed so soon by the loss of my brother, combined with the recognition that I had now left New Zealand and wouldn't be going back to live there again, brought me to a standstill. My usual strong sense of direction and motivation deserted me and this was bewildering as I have always been driven by the creative impulse to make a difference. I felt disoriented, as if I'd been spun around in the dark in a game of blind man's buff and was staggering, dazed and whirling, in an unfamiliar world.

The Healing Process

It is our willingness to deeply feel our human heartbreak and to allow
the emotional energy to flow through us that brings about changes in
our behaviour. And yet heartbreak is often accompanied by habitual
judgments which interrupt the flow of energy and keep us stuck in old
patterns. As we build the skill of witnessing our suffering while releasing
habitual judgments, we enable healing to happen more easily.

David's death stirred me to reflect deeply on our family dynamics and opened the possibility for healing. I think of healing as the restoration of the natural flow of life's energy. During the course of an ordinary day you may be moved to reach out and touch another person with love, or you may spontaneously burst into song, or cry out with frustration, you may melt into tears of sorrow or feel moved to curl up and go to sleep. However, if your life experience has taught you that it is not safe to love, or you will be punished when you sing, that you shouldn't make a fuss and it's lazy to rest during the day, you will have learned to block the natural flow of your life force by contracting your body and your mind. Additionally, you will have developed the habit of numbing or comforting yourself. As a child you may have used sweet foods, as an adult cigarettes or alcohol. Learning to control emotions and impulses is a normal part of the socialisation process – it would be a chaotic world if everyone was indiscriminately touching, singing, crying and sleeping – but when the process of self-control has been accompanied by shame, harsh criticism or violence, the interruptions to the natural flow of self-expression may be deeply held and unconscious. Some of these will have been passed on from generation to generation.

As I grieved for my brother, I held a container for the tangled web of my emotions: a profound sense of injustice at his loss, remorse at how I could have behaved better, a haunting sense of aloneness, a deep sense of inadequacy, stretched me at times beyond the limits of what I felt I could bear. During this period of healing I evolved the practice I call "sitting with death and choosing life" to help me through these complex feelings. This is a simple yet powerful practice of being fully present with whatever is arising in experience, while at the same time witnessing thoughts and emotions from the unconditionally loving perspective of a spiritual being. In other words we can develop the capacity to experience both the vulnerability of our human being and the love and wisdom of the soul at the same time. This is a bit like remembering to have a torch with you when you enter a shadowy room. The light may deepen the shadows and yet you have a source of comfort with you at all times.

Adopting a Simple Transformational Practice

Our human experience takes place within an animal, sentient body in which we are driven, often unconsciously, by desires, instincts and emotions. The boundary of the skin around the body can give rise to a sense of separation, but in the West, where individuality and a strong sense of identity are highly prized, it is the mind rather than the body that separates us from others. We live within a culture that has conditioned us to behave in certain ways in order to fit in and be accepted. The conditioned mind is like a cloudy sky hanging over and veiling our true authentic nature. These clouds of the conditioned mind are torn apart when death or shock wakes us up and the light of our essential being breaks through, even if only for a moment. Our inner light reveals whatever has been hidden in the shadows and those parts of the self we have exiled, out of shame or guilt, are revealed. This can add to the experience of shock but we then have the choice to welcome these fragments of our being back into the community of the unconditional heart.

During a healing process we naturally experience many different emotions intensely and, when we have habitually used judgments to avoid these emotions and push away the pain of loss, our natural flow of energy is interrupted. Much of our human suffering is kept alive by self-judgments and judgments of others which are so deeply embedded in the psyche we don't even notice them. "I shouldn't be feeling like this." "I should be over this by now." "There must be something terribly wrong with me." "Oh, I behaved so badly." This constant stream of self-criticism can limit our consciousness and choices so that we lose touch with our natural wisdom, our instincts and love of life, and then we don't experience the good things in life as fully. Over time, energy becomes clogged and stagnant resulting in poor mental and physical health. By choosing to become aware of our judgments and refusing to be controlled by them we become more present to whatever we are feeling here and now. As we open to receive the messages from our emotions we realise they are simply part of our life force arising to show us more of who we are. Then we may realise just how much energy is required to repress and keep certain emotions out of awareness and under wraps. This simple process of noticing, becoming aware and making choices is a transformational practice which, over time, brings great benefits. We can bring more kindness and compassion into our self-care, release fear and resistance and allow the flow of life to move through us. Then we experience more peace, spaciousness, joy and compassion – more unity with people and life.

Physical and mental pain point to an imbalance and warn us that we may be holding the energy of disturbing emotions too tightly and that some emotion is crying out to be expressed, heard and released. In my practice of sitting with death and choosing life, as I notice an imbalance I can choose to relax, give space to the emotional energy and experience it, allowing it to flow through me and move me. I receive information from the emotions and a wave of life force is freed to complete its momentum. For example, the heavy energy of remorse may be telling me I wish I had behaved differently and that something better is possible. It is not an invitation to beat myself up for being a bad person or to descend into a lengthy depression but instead it can be seen an as an opportunity to be more aware, conscious and loving from this moment on. Anger may be telling me that someone has crossed a boundary and I'm feeling exploited and frustrated with myself for allowing it to happen. By giving inner space to the fiery energy of anger and allowing it to release in a safe way, the energy magically transforms. This in turn motivates me to find the courage, and develop the skill, to draw clear boundaries.

Some of us interrupt the flow of life force at the point when the emotions arise. Others, who have become habituated to "processing" may become overly identified with their pain and get bogged down in remorse and sadness, replaying the old story of "if only.." over and over. When we make an identity out of our suffering it can become an uncomfortable comfort zone to which we cling rather than taking the risks involved in moving forward and opening to life.

It's important to remember that some of the old beliefs and behaviour patterns that still drive us today were adopted a long time ago in order to keep us safe. When new information enters and it's time to make a change, this challenges our old ways of adapting and may even feel life-threatening. For me, the letting go of suffering, inner conflict and tension happens, not by any act of will but at the point when I feel most helpless and unable to keep holding on to the old beliefs and behaviours. Then there is the involuntary relaxation of surrender - a letting go that brings sweet relief as it releases me to be held within the free, expansive, unconditioned, loving space of soul. Fully here, now, in the body, experiencing, welcoming and witnessing everything arising, held within this expanded space, I know the joy of liberation. Everything that has seemed difficult and painful now appears to be simply another opportunity to realise who I truly am and what this human life is for.

Practice: Becoming an Unconditionally Loving Container for All Your Emotions

An important aspect of grieving is to grow the skills of welcoming your entire inner community of competing emotions, beliefs, prejudices, virtues, strengths and limitations. As you grieve for another's sorrow and suffering, and your own, and you allow the energy of grief to move through you, you can become a conscious container to witness and embrace it all. You are at once both the still strength of the container - the witnessing soul or unconditionally loving spiritual being, and the turbulent movement of the emotions - the evolving human being. By holding the tension between these two aspects of the Self, you can heal and redeem the power that has been trapped within your suffering. You can transmute the pain you are holding by becoming aware of those beliefs and judgments that no longer serve loving consciousness. You can absorb from your experience what is good and nourishing, chew over what is indigestible and spit out those beliefs you no longer need. As you develop the capacity to include and embrace your losses and failures, and acknowledge where you have been broken, you can let go, make space, expand, transform and move on.

Part one: Being Present with Everything That Arises

Earlier, on page 34, I gave you a practice for raising awareness of your feelings as they arise. I invite you to return to this now and extend it.

Starting with five minutes every morning simply sit quietly, close your eyes and notice whatever is arising within you. For example:

Now I'm aware of the breath and I notice I am breathing into my chest..
Now I'm aware of a tension around my heart..
Now I can feel tears behind my eyes and I'm tightening my eyes to keep them back..
Now I'm clenching my fists..
Now I'm getting frustrated and telling myself I'm stupid..
Now I'm feeling uncomfortable and want to run away..
Just notice and keep breathing.

As you become accustomed to the practice extend the time to ten minutes, fifteen, thirty.
Then try doing the practice when you are feeling agitated or upset.

At the end of each practice thank yourself for being willing.

Part Two: Developing the Unconditionally Loving Witness

Begin by bringing all your awareness into your breath and, breathing gently, follow the breath with your awareness, all the way in and all the way out.

As you start to feel calm imagine that you have a deep well of peace at the centre of your being. You can come and drink at this well whenever you please. Imagine the well now. Is it a small pond with crystal clear water that you can sip from and see your face reflected back to you? Is it an old stone structure with a wooden bucket that you can lower into the dark water beneath? See your own inner wellspring and drink from it. As the water touches your lips taste its freshness and imagine pure spring water circulating throughout your body energising you and waking you up.

Now breathe that calm, reviving energy throughout your body until your whole being is filled with peaceful, life giving, loving energy. Does this energy have a colour? Imagine you're being filled with the beautiful colour of unconditional love. This is a love that accepts you totally. Every fibre of your being is seen and loved. Can you allow yourself to receive this now?

The more you practice being in the presence of the unconditional love that always resides in the core of your being, the more easily you will be able to call on this source of renewal when you are going through troubled times.

The next time you are starting to judge or criticise yourself harshly, remember the wellspring, recall the colour of your loving energy, and breathe it through your being.

You can listen to this meditation by going to the free resources on this webpage: https://www.tribeintransition.net/a-story-of-transformation-free-resources/

Submit to Being Stripped to the Bone

> *The Dark Night of the Soul is an inescapable event when walking*
> *the spiritual path. At various stages in one's spiritual development, a*
> *sense of inner blindness will inevitably emerge. When strong, it leads*
> *to the feeling of spiritual abandonment. The wisdom and direction*
> *of the soul disappears, and we are forced to face the darkness of our*
> *life predicament without an inner light to show the way. Yet in truth,*
> *it is a darkness that emerges before the soul's dawning hour.*
> William Meader[2]

There comes a point in the transformational process when the personality that has carried us this far is too small to hold the energy of the growing self. Think of the growing self as a plant that needs repotting. When roots begin to poke through the bottom of the pot and the leaves begin to wilt it's time to lift the plant out of its old home and give it a new, more spacious container. The same is true for the growing self; at a certain point it's necessary to risk the vulnerability of letting go of the old, limited identity so that we can expand into a new, more integrated self. This may include letting go, at least temporarily, of aspects of the self that we are very attached to. For me, writing, teaching, visioning and innovating have long been transformational tools and part of my consciousness practice. Creativity has been the magical ingredient I could always rely on to get me through and find sense in otherwise barren times. I forged an identity around my creativity believing this is who I am. When I am in the flow of inspiration I feel expanded, energised and clear about of my direction in life and sure of what I am here to do. At the same time, I've come to know the spiritual path to be a slow and steady peeling away of the layers of the personality - who I think I am - in order that I can discover who I truly am as an embodied soul. As a conscious healer committed to transforming consciousness I know it is necessary at times to submit to being stripped to the bone, and then from ground zero, to grow in authenticity beyond ego and the desires of the personality, into service to something bigger.

So much had already been peeled away, I had been expecting and dreading for years the apparent ending of my creative liveliness. I'd had an uneasy feeling it was inevitable that at some point my creative gifts would be eclipsed and I didn't know how I would survive without them. Now, in this deepening of the labour of grief, sure enough, the wellspring of inspiration dried up and I was incapable of writing anything at all. I had no choice but to sit with the dying of the self that had carried me this far. I understood then, with a deeper knowing than before, that the healing and evolution of humanity starts with my own conscious healing and the embodiment of authentic truth and that letting go of the outgrown identity is essential to this process.

To sit with death is to take a direction diametrically opposed to that of our culture, like a salmon swimming upstream to the deathing-birthing place. In that sense, it is radically counter-cultural. The forces that drive mainstream Western culture keep alive the old paradigm that is killing life and encourage a state of restlessness, desire, wanting, a sense of lack, cultivation of image, distraction, striving and accumulation. The psyche that drives our world has been fashioned by the engine of commerce and the consumer society to be goal-oriented and self-centred. We see the consequences of this self-absorbed mentality in the devastation of nature as a ruthlessly plundered resource and in the destruction of diverse cultures through war, theft of land, genocide and other forms of domination which break communities and uproot people and animals from their homelands.

To sit with death is to encounter stillness, silence, emptiness, absence of desire. It is to be with a power much bigger than the self, in the face of which one has no choice but to suffer the falling away of everything within that no longer serves life. Rather like a tree in autumn, the life force is withdrawn from the stems and the old leaves are destined to fall, to make space for the new season's growth to come. And yet, in the falling of the leaves, there is no consoling thought of a future spring. There is, maybe, a distant memory of renewal but otherwise the future is unimaginable. There is only this present moment, this emptiness.

Being human isn't easy. Learning how to look life and death fully in the face without illusion, and then to move beyond judgment into unconditional love, takes commitment. Sitting with death is a kind of detox process, a fasting from the pleasures and distractions of the world.

Held within the grey stones of my ramshackle cottage, as the poisons of old beliefs and wounds were released to be transformed and healed, I felt smelly and foul and unfit for company. I naturally hunkered towards solitude, hiding in my cave while I licked my wounds clean. With everything covered in the dust and grit of deconstruction, I had no appetite, nothing was fresh and juicy. I became a dried-out husk hanging on the tree of life and I couldn't recognise this shrivelled being as myself.

Surely this must be how it is to die? The slow decomposing of the body, the loss of functions, the narrowing of the world, the struggle to transform the rotting fruit into an offering for the gods. And emotionally, the parade of remorse and regrets, the striving to reach acceptance and forgiveness, to atone and become at one with life. This is the challenge to which death calls us: to accept even this indignity and the loss of everything we hold dear.

As layers of illusion, outworn beliefs, certainties and outgrown small versions of self were let go, I experienced disorientation alternating with joyful glimpses of liberation. I had tasted emptiness before – both the peace of limitless eternal time and the fear of being lost and alone in this vastness. Previously, I had chosen not to stay too long there, in the unbounded unknown. Instead, I'd dive back into the stream of life and hitch a ride on the next wave of inspiration. For instance, in the event I told you earlier, when the house I was living in with Maggie was damaged by flood and landslide, the experience was a mini death, a tearing of the veils, and we both chose to use the apparent disaster to make a transformational leap into a more expanded perspective. About six weeks after the event, as we were recuperating on a remote island in the Marlborough Sounds, I was faced with a choice: either I could go further into the expansive space of not-knowing, which was opening inside me and explore further or, I could get back to work. I chose to get back to work and launched a new teleseminar series called True Wealth, running backwards and forwards to secure the internet connection on our remote outpost so that I could hold the calls. Yet intuitively I knew, at some point in my spiritual adventure of deepening into soul, I would lose this creative outlet and be obliged to sit with whatever unfinished business my busy-ness was hiding. That moment of reckoning had now arrived.

In those months of spring and summer, as my labour of grief progressed, it was strange to get up in the morning with nothing calling me to action. With my connection to inspiration obscured, I had no purpose, no motivation, no hope, no joy. Now, apparently, I had to learn how to live without these spiritual staples. I was experiencing the stark emptiness of being stripped of all comfort, to the core of my sense of self. Creativity had provided me with identity and purpose, made sense of my life and constructed a future. With creativity gone, my future also disappeared.

So, who was I now? Honestly, I didn't recognise myself. I was helpless in the face of this psychic stripping and there was nothing I could do. I was reduced to *this* moment and it was not a light and open presence but a now heavy with the fatigue of the past. I dragged my body around, doing only what had to be done. I fed myself, kept the house tidy, wrote essential emails. It was summer but I barely went out to admire the day or to allow the sun to kiss my skin. I woke late and by 3pm was prone on the couch surfing the TV channels for some entertainment. This was so unlike me. I simply didn't know myself.

I felt so weighed down and, at the same time, this stifling weight felt like emptiness and lack. It crossed my mind that perhaps my tiredness was the accumulation of a lifetime's effort from carrying the heavy burden of responsibility for my family, and for the world, pushing myself ever onwards. Perhaps this emptiness was the beginning of the unravelling of this burden? Maybe freedom was not far away but I couldn't touch it yet.

For the transformational healing of grief to be completed I had to find the courage to face into the darkness and look. What I saw was a bound prisoner, submitting as the layers of illusion were peeled away. And although this hurt with the pain of a bandage suddenly stripped from the skin, I had to keep on looking until the untruths, the half-truths, the faulty beliefs, the limiting habits, had all been witnessed and set free.

Eventually I began to feel a new space emerging and the scent of fresh air flowed in.

Whether you've sailed the world in a yacht, climbed Everest, or sung solo in front of a full auditorium, this turning to face your own truth takes more courage, I guarantee it.

These two poems explore this deconstruction of the old self which lives at the centre of the transformational process.

Let Go

On a wave, rise up, and see!

Everything looks friendly and smells of fresh salt air

then

tip over the edge and slide

down the sheer green side

of the reckless ocean

not fighting to claim life but

surrendering

until

the self is obliterated

stripped apart bit by bit

and there is nothing left to hold onto

and no one left to hold

only

this intense dissolving into no-thingness

this living on the edge of life and death

where

some essential rawness holds the power

to consume whatever remains

of the dying self

there is nowhere beyond this moment

everything else is fiction

Rose Diamond

only this moment

lived with the fullness and intensity of a child

not a single drop of experience squandered

now

at one with

the raw charge of life energy

free to evaporate into the mist

and touch the dynamic sky

through which the universe is playing

Rose Diamond, from *Songs of Awakening*[3]

Enter the Great Re-Cycling

Confined in a small space without an exit
suspended in a sleepy hammock with no choice
a lazy soporific drug has been poured into my brain
my mind is full of holes and the darkness of space.
Words escape into oblivion
nothing connects
reality is flattened and reduced
and everything collapses into the debris of deconstruction.
There are no possibilities beyond this.

At times a pulse pushes against my skin
refuses the downward pull of entropy
while frozen faces locked in habit
appear as taunting ghouls in a hallucinogenic dream
demanding attention, love and friendship
insist on being seen
then melt
like icebergs on a doomed planet
returning to the ocean
evaporating into the clouds.

And yet amidst this disappearing act
something watches, something knows
something strong and unbreakable
something soft, yielding and fluent

something ancient holding hands with something new.

Rose Diamond, from *Songs of Awakening* [4]

What Happens to Consciousness After the Body Dies?

> *It is in this willingness to shed inflexible and limiting ideas of who we are that the evolution of humanity lies. In time, I discovered that what I thought was emptiness is actually a source of love, alive with possibilities and full of gifts. In the act of sitting with death, we may discover our ability to deepen our love, our understanding and our compassion for what it is to be human. Then we can expand our possibilities as we consciously choose to be creative participants in life.*

Over a lifetime, as we cast off personalities that have grown too small to encompass all that we are becoming, there is a steady light in us that endures. This is the light we can always reach for when we are troubled. At the end of each soul chapter we don't so much re-invent ourselves, because this doesn't happen by an act of will, but the light that we are shapes the next embodiment of our story, guided by our soul choices and supported by our skills. This shedding of skins helps to develop an attitude of non-attachment which prepares us for the bigger letting go of death.

David experienced this evolution of the self, no matter how briefly. He'd burst onto his new stage in the village where he'd bought his land, open hearted and full of enthusiasm to share his plans. In response, everyone he met warmed to him and saw him as a "lovely man". I saw his death as both a tragedy and a victory all rolled up in one. He was a fruit that fell from the tree the moment it reaches its fullness.

As the one left behind, the death of a loved one can awaken and move us into a renewed life story. By attempting to journey with David as best I could into the afterlife, on the wings of imagination and music, I was able to expand my consciousness and my perspective of what is possible.

There is a growing body of testimony from people who have had near death experiences, which points to a first stage of dying, before the life review, in which the one departing the body moves towards a radiant and powerful white light glowing with love and welcome. For many people there is comfort in this testimony and a taste of unconditional love and perfection. I believe these are simply the first few steps on a long journey into a mystery we cannot know for sure. It is the mystery of how consciousness evolves, the mystery of Soul and human destiny, and of our place in the grand design of Cosmos. When we can face death and life in a very open-minded way, with beginner's mind, not reaching for easy comfort, but coming to rest in a place of not knowing, we are free to receive the many rich and unexpected gifts available to us here and now.

In the last few weeks of Woods' life, I read about and researched into the afterlife and talked with him about it. To the end he maintained a healthy, open scepticism admitting he didn't know and was unwilling to be confined within any comforting illusion; he remained a free spirit to the last.

My understanding of the afterlife is forever evolving and I really don't have any definite answers to the mystery that is death but I am sure consciousness goes on and cannot be destroyed. Until very recently I have had no evidence that the accumulated wisdom and karma carried by an individual continues in any recognisable form. None of my departed loved ones has ever communicated with me in an unambiguous way to lead me to believe they are "still there" in a separate form. I imagine the personality is shaken off, along with the outworn body, as being now too small and inadequate a vehicle for the soul's ongoing journey. Perhaps the accumulated skills, wisdom and knowledge, as well as whatever is yet to be transformed, is integrated into the bigger multi-dimensional space of Soul. In this way the consciousness we have accrued in this lifetime exists beyond time and the physical realm where it continues to evolve and to support human evolution, as and where required. Perhaps the personality remains available as one of many possible garments the journeying soul can wear, so that it can communicate with those left behind on Earth. I'm sure the soul also has many more new, exciting possibilities to explore and I have heard that, for those in advanced stages of enlightenment, consciousness outgrows even the soul and that faithful companion has to be let go too. Maybe our loved ones simply live on within us. I don't have answers to these existential questions but I do know, in consciousness there is no separation between past and future, here and there, me and you. All life is One.

One of the ideas that appealed to me in my reading was that, after the life review, the soul travels beyond time and space, as we know it on Earth, to join a familiar "soul family" with whom we continue our practice of expanding consciousness. When I read this, I had a comforting feeling that many of the things I hold dear here and now, like soul friendship and deep discovery conversations, are happening even more fully "on the other side" and life and death are simply a continuum. For a while this made me yearn to leave and follow Woods and David into the spirit world. But in the end, I realised my calling is to remain here and play my part on Earth.

When I attempt to keep a very open and free mind and resist comforting solutions, I also play with the possibility that death is in fact the end. When the loved one's gone, they are gone. When I go, I will be gone. Into what? Into nothingness, into the great unknown, the cloud of unknowing. No more "me", no more "you". Pouf! Just like that. What happens when you open to this possibility? Can you take it in? And what difference does it make to the way you live now if you think the soul goes on, or if you think death is the end?

As he was preparing to leave his body, Woods and I talked about how we would communicate after he'd gone.

He said, "I'm not sure how it works over there, Rosy. But, of course, I will if I can. But how will I find you?"

My confident reply, "I'll find you", surprised him.

I'm looking for you now, Woods.

Where do we go after we die? Does this identity, this Earth being, return home to a bigger soul family? Do we join all our many incarnations, past and future, out there, beyond time, co-existing in simultaneous space?

Or do we merge into nothingness and become one with the vast unknown?

It is a stretch, almost too much to bear, to consider you gone and to think we will never meet again. To know that I too will disappear one day and be likewise lost to the world.

Where are you Woods? Where are you David? Can you feel me? Can you hear me? As I am hold my memories of you and remember your love, I look up into the sky to find you in the clouds and the response to my questions clearly comes:

"All the answers are written in nature. Allow the present moment to bring you everything you need."

Chapter Six

Transformation

Gather Your Tools for Transformation

There is always a sense that, through the creative process at its best, I open to a force much bigger and wiser than my limited personality. As I connect with the creative impulse I become a vessel through which a powerful force for good can flow, find form and be seeded into the collective consciousness. My job has been to learn how to co-create with this inspired, intelligent energy.

I find it beautiful that our greatest challenges and sorrows can become the source of our deepest meaning, purpose and creative expression. Throughout this book I have been offering you a map of sorts and a series of skills and practices you can use to transform grief into healing and find your way to a new life story. To be motivated you have to believe that transformation is possible and that you can work with the dull lead of your experience and transform it into gold. If you have ever built or refurbished a house; made a garden; taken a project from seed idea to a final report of progress; carried, given birth to and raised a child; written a book; painted a picture; or any number of other creative activities, then you know what it means to take raw materials and transform them into something which didn't exist before. You already have many skills, a rich resource of life experience, an inner knowing, an instinct for what is needed and a fund of courage and ingenuity.

Then you need a vehicle for transformation. We all have our own favourite vehicles and I've introduced mine throughout the book: writing, inquiry, deep discovery conversations, bringing exploratory groups together and creating educational projects. What are yours?

I've come to see the three life streams of grieving, healing and creativity as inextricably linked. From its first upwelling in my life, writing poetry revealed my soul and became my vehicle for transformation. Writing takes me deeply into my own experience and then opens the door into transpersonal understandings and connections. It is the way I connect with my soul purpose and with the human family.

Writing, for me, is very compelling. It's a vehicle for bringing a bigger energy and intelligence through my being. I have never called this "channelling" and yet there is always a sense that through the creative process, at its best, I open to a force much bigger and wiser than my limited personality. As I connect with the creative impulse I become a vessel through which a powerful force for good can flow and then find form and be seeded into the collective consciousness. My job has been to learn how to co-create with this inspired, intelligent energy, which I have called variously soul, Soul and the evolutionary impulse. In my understanding soul is a treasure trove of personal wisdom which carries our individual story, gifts, history, karma, potential and destiny. Soul is a species Over Soul which carries our collective story, gifts, history, karma, potential and destiny. The evolutionary impulse is the creative life force broadcasting new ideas and possibilities like seeds in an infinite and inexhaustible flow of intelligence that is always available. When we are connected with our personal soul, and with the species Soul, and we open to the evolutionary impulse, we can create a future which is at once new and innovative and rooted in the accumulated wisdom of the past.

The primary skill that has supported me through all my creative activities is deep listening, which is closely linked to intuition. Right now, as I sit here at my computer on this winter's day, I am sensing into my being with the intention of bringing forth the wisdom that is here. I'm holding my memories and personal experiences and listening for the underlying patterns and truths that are calling to be expressed through me. I see this as a co-creative conversation between personality (me) and my deeply knowing soul. When I also introduce the skill of inquiry this makes the conversation even more lively. As soon as I am able to clarify my question - a question that is vitally important to me - the answers start to come. Throughout the day, I pick up a book and read a paragraph that lights up my understanding, I have a conversation with someone who brings me insight with their own threads of experience, or I have a dream. When I'm writing a book, I'm listening for the underlying form and flow which may not be revealed all at once. It's more like a weaving as I go back and forth many times to weave in a bit more information here, a fresh insight there.

Ever since I started to write poetry my life has been an ongoing conversation with soul. This has brought me inner riches beyond anything I could have thought up and has always left me feeling one of the most blessed and privileged people on Earth.

Allow Your Soul Work to Emerge Through You

When I talk about our "soul work" I am referring to the soul choices we have made which call us to realise who we are essentially, to develop our soul qualities, to redeem our gifts from the shadows, and to put our gifts in service to the healing and wholing of our world.

In that beautiful summer spring and summer of 2020, I was living with peace and sunshine in my little piece of heaven between the mountains of Snowdonia and the waters of Cardigan Bay, while in the bigger world all around the pandemic was raging and people were dying and afraid. Then a quiet power tapped me on the shoulder and asked me if I was willing to take up the task of spreading grief awareness. I knew this project had my name on it and I said YES and my yes landed softly in my body and took root. From that moment I was committed to the evolution of the *Sitting with Death and Choosing Life Programme* and I took up my mission to educate, encourage, empower and equip people to move through grief, towards a fulfilling participation in community life. This commitment has required me to bring my whole being to the creative process - all my energy, devotion and experience - and it has provided me with the opportunity to bring together all the skills and wisdom of a lifetime in an act of integration and completion. This has been immensely rich and fulfilling and has challenged me to draw forth all my determination, resilience and commitment.

With any major creative project, whether it's writing a book or creating an educational programme, I have a sense of putting myself in service to a greater intelligence. From the start, *The Sitting with Death and Choosing Life Programme*, had a life and direction of its own and I felt it to be divinely inspired. The work became a compelling relationship, a partnership, a love affair with Soul which I was called to serve.

The process of birthing a big project into the world beautifully illustrates the dilemmas of a spiritual being having a human experience. To bring a vision down to earth means developing the art of translating the vision into words and actions so that human experience can be uplifted towards the realisation of the vision. It is necessary to attend to both higher values and human needs simultaneously.

Hold the Creative Tension

Creative tension inevitably arises in any emergent project that is headed somewhere. With the *Sitting with Death and Choosing Life Programme*, a global vision for a more humane world and faith in the evolution of consciousness, are the big container for the project. This includes an open-eyed recognition of our life-threatening collective human problems and an acknowledgment of the magnitude of the task we face collectively to redeem life. A vision of how grief awareness can open the heart and transform society sits side by side with the day to day challenges of holding people through grief and living with my own grief while empowering others. Within these tensions, I have lived the question of how to stay creatively vibrant as I do my soul work, developing the skills to be responsive, experimental and co-operative alongside being focused and determined. I do my best to practice what I'm preaching by being still, receptive and listening deeply. I know, despite the urgency of our existential crises, people move at their own pace, the transformational process can't be hurried and I need to be patient, diligent and discerning.

The project has emerged, grown, evolved and had its own momentum, which I have been called to serve. I brought my first group together in the autumn of 2020 around a course which was an experiment with content and methodology, like a sketch or framework upon which a work of art is woven. By 2022 this first course had become differentiated into an eco-system of five interconnected courses, including a training for empowering facilitators.[1] I had no plan to build in this way but as soon as I had designed and piloted one course the seed idea for the next one presented. I have felt compelled to construct something which can eventually be independent of me as I hold a big vision for the spread of this work which cannot be fulfilled by one person alone.

I have worked the hardest I have ever worked in my life, firing on all cylinders - writing materials, creating courses, recruiting participants and running courses, driven by an urgent need for completion. I've been holding many tensions within the creative process: the time pressure of our collective predicaments; the desire to equip and empower people to meet these creatively; the urgency created by the prospect of diminishing life force in older age; and a compelling desire to gather and pass on all the skills and wisdom from my lifetime as a whole person educator, change agent, and archaeologist of soul. Even as I am committed to completing and delivering the programme, I also sense there is something more beyond this that I am hungry to experience. And so, I move forward, tending the seeds of my grief as they keep growing, blossoming and putting out fruit.

In addition to the tensions I have already mentioned, there is also a tension between the two different kinds of consciousness: the more goal oriented, focussed, linear consciousness (often referred to as the Masculine principle) and the more diffuse, receptive, intuitive inner knowing (the Feminine principle). This balancing act intersects with the tension around time; with the work emerging in its own time, taking its own time to develop, and requiring deep listening and patience; held side by side with a sense of global urgency. Holding, containing and resolving these tensions is a vital part of the transformational process and essential to the evolution of consciousness as we progress towards our next integral stage.

I can't claim to be an expert at holding creative tension and every new creative experience presents new challenges. It is not my experience, as some people assert, that when I am in creative flow, life is always easy. I value the poet, dreamer and visionary in me and I love to float in the timeless space of liminal consciousness; indeed, I believe this is essential to my well-being, and to the well-being of us all. I also believe there is a place for effort and sometimes it's necessary to strive to move beyond conditioned limitations to get the thing done. An essential part of the practice of conscious creating is discerning when to push through resistance and pursue the creative goals of a project, and when to stop, listen, surrender and enter into deep, liminal space to await new directions. I have had a tendency in the past, when under pressure, to put my head down, push on through and ignore my deeper needs. The skill is in finding the balance between the yin of free-floating, receptive consciousness and the yang of focused momentum. This requires returning often to a place of equilibrium and non-attachment – to beginner's mind - and listening again. Learning to develop and balance these skills is essential for those of us on a conscious path who want to co-operate with whatever is emerging at the edge of consciousness.

None of us creates alone. The skills and experience I have brought to this project have evolved over a lifetime and are the integrated gifts of the many people who have guided and influenced me. My ability to improve all the courses and bring them into a completed form has been a result of the participation and feedback of all involved, including the Emergence Foundation who supported me with a grant.[2] Participating with others in deep inquiry is a privilege and a responsibility which keeps me accountable and grows me as a leader. My personal exploration anchors me into the earth of our common humanity and our collective history; it embeds me into the web of life. At the same time, my mind is open and receptive and I am being guided every step of the way.

Remember We Are in a Collective Process of Transition

The autumn of 2021 brought a noticeable shift in energy in my groups which appeared to reflect a bigger movement in the collective consciousness. It was as if we were all trudging through mud, with every forward step taking a huge effort. We kept showing up and attempting to find words to communicate our experience and each of us was a voice articulating a piece of the bigger story of humanity's transition, or dark night of the soul. This is a transition in which we have left the safe and known of the past and yet we have no idea what the future will hold, and increasingly we doubt if there will be a future. Each of us, in our own way was in the process of identity shift, in which the beliefs we had lived by were no longer fit for purpose and the light that had illuminated our way forward had dimmed. We had entered the valley of the shadow of death together and there were no guarantees we would emerge back into the light. And yet, as a community of conscious healers, we were sure of the value of journeying together through this process of discovery. Even though we met in virtual reality, from different corners of the UK, when we were together we were connected and that connection became our sanctuary, our safe space, our little island of sanity.

At the centre of the Sitting with Death and Choosing Life Programme, and at the centre of this book, is encouragement to adopt simple practices which can support you to live in a more expanded, inspired, loving consciousness, more of the time. These practices are simple but not easy. I'm encouraging you to fly in the face of considerable disempowerment, built over centuries, and to follow your longing to transcend this. You may recognise the need to create a bigger, more uplifted energy field with others and to gather skills to go beyond the egoic mind, the self-interested needs of "me". By listening deeply to what is arising to be expressed, not just for the sake of your own individual self-expression, but as your best contribution to the emerging conversation, you will open to new ideas and inspirations, connect into our common humanity and serve our interconnectedness.[3]

I feel deeply privileged to be part of this process and, as challenging as it has been, I know the value of the meetings with my groups goes beyond the group itself. Our willingness to come together and witness each other through this transition of consciousness gives rise to a growing understanding of what it means to be human. It is part of the soul work we have been called together to do as conscious healers. This deeper sense of meaning and connection has kept me going through the travails of the transformational process.

My programme was one of many initiatives drawing people together into exploratory groups during the very challenging time of the pandemic. Many people gathered under the umbrella of Extinction Rebellion[3] or Death Cafes[4] using the internet to connect. When I imagine the many thousands of people meeting in this way throughout the UK, and many hundreds of thousands more around the world, my faith in conscious evolution is kept alive. Although the internet can be used for immoral purposes, for many of us during this time of physical isolation, it has truly been a lifeline.

Transmute Suffering

We can transmute suffering by being present to whatever arises. Suffering is part of the human condition and the conditions for human suffering have been passed down from generation to generation over thousands of years of evolution. As His Holiness the Dalai Lama has said, "all humans long to be happy and all humans suffer." In our current epoch, our materialistic, consumption-driven western culture feeds the desire mind with the idea that if we just have this thing, that experience, this ideal companion, then we will be happy. When we are not happy, we think there is something wrong with us and that we must be unlovable; or we judge there is something wrong with others, or with the world. It is an essential skill to learn how to give ourselves fully to painful emotions arising within us, and to feel into our own personal shortcomings *and at the same time*, to hold a bigger perspective and to realise that the feelings flowing through us are transpersonal and shared by most humans. It is this skilful holding together of the personal, alongside the transpersonal perspective, that enables the evolution of consciousness and collective healing.

Grief is a powerful process with a life of its own. This practice of sitting with death and choosing life - giving grief all the space it needs, being with whatever arises and then to keep choosing life - is similar to a meditation or a mindfulness practice. Through being with our grief fully, we develop the awareness, strength and ability to be totally present and engaged with life. The practice opens a space around the events of the individual life story and, in time, loosens identification with either the victories or the unhappiness we have experienced. We move into a new state of equilibrium or equanimity where we are not taking life events so personally. As we stay with this process of transmutation we are gifted with the arising of wisdom, acceptance, forgiveness and compassion. Through grieving we come to realise more of our essential humanness and by doing so we become kinder and more tolerant towards the human condition as it appears in ourselves and in others.

When I worked as a gestalt therapist, many people who came to me were afraid of their own grief. They feared that if they started crying they'd never stop, that they would be engulfed, overwhelmed and destroyed by grief. Indeed, when I started doing my own therapy, I cried for months alone in my room sobbing, and often I didn't know why. A river of sadness flowed through me and I was just sad, I didn't have to know why and I did stop crying eventually.

As we fully allow our grief, something *is* destroyed, some old sense of self, some habitual place to hide we've constructed to protect us and which is no longer needed. But the essential self, the core of who we really are, is strengthened through this process of deconstruction. I came to call this recurring cycle of descent into grief, "bottoming out". With each descent and renewal, I grow stronger and I learn that I can contain the pain and it won't kill me. By holding grief in the crucible of the body, feeling it fully, witnessing and accepting the experience, trusting and surrendering to its power, the core of the essential self grows stronger and brighter.

And now, here I am, the last one standing in my family, on the front line, nowhere to hide.

Chapter Seven

Choosing Life

Harvest the Fruits of the Conscious Healing Process

As I've been writing, I've discovered untold riches within the apparent tragedy of death and loss. I've seen more deeply into my own story and realised the role I had taken on as the family healer was not the burden I had felt it to be but an opportunity to learn and grow, to find meaning and self-actualisation within suffering and to receive fulfilment through being of service.

And now we come to the harvest. As we gather the gifts of grieving, healing and transforming, we complete with our grief and integrate what we have discovered through sitting with death, so that we may move on wholeheartedly into a renewed story. This is an essential part of the work of Soul, which carries the grand design of human purpose and conscious evolution. Soul calls us to be all we can be and to offer our gifts into the world, not for any hope of personal gain, but because this is what we are here to do and where we find fulfilment.

Your Soul Basket

When everything has been stripped away
and you stand naked before the door
When the world is reduced to one point
and there is no longer a choice
Gather your wisdom into your soul basket

harvest the fruits of experience
polish them on your sleeve
pile the basket high
and walk courageously toward the door
trusting it will open.

Offer your contribution
with no expectation of return
because this is who you are
and why you're here
and what you have to give.

Rose Diamond, from *Songs of Awakening,*[1]

Writing this book has been a work of transformation which I began as a way to come to know grief and to support myself through a troubled time of personal loss. I have used many words in my attempt to come to know aspects of human experience that defy words – the loss of a loved one, the essence of another human being, the mysteries of the inner world, the profound suffering of humanity. In the face of all of this words are inadequate. And yet I have been compelled to stay with the challenge and I've allowed it to stretch me mentally, emotionally and spiritually, leading me ever more deeply into the healing process, where there is always another layer to delve into, always more to know and see. The work has led me to places I thought I was finished with and invited me to look again.

So here I am in the middle way....
Trying to learn to use words, and every attempt
Is a wholly new start, and a different kind of failure
Because one has only learnt to get the better of words
For the things one no longer has to say, or the way in which
One is no longer disposed to say it. And so each venture
Is a new beginning, a raid on the inarticulate ...
For us, there is only the trying. The rest is not our business.

T.S. Eliot, East Coker from Four Quartets[2]

My book has been the transformational container or alchemical vessel in which my personal sorrow has been distilled and transmuted until now there are only gifts remaining and I am experiencing a harvest of quiet joy and knowing. I hope sharing my harvest will encourage you to keep moving forward through your own troubled times, making the choice for conscious healing and wholeness, until your grief has been transformed.

As I stand at the threshold of a new soul chapter here are some of the gifts I bring:

Freedom from the Fear of Death

*I've discovered how death, as well as being a source
of heartbreak, may also be a victory.*

The mass denial of death which has shaped our world is also a denial of life. Until we are able to accept and honour death as a natural part of life, and to acknowledge the inevitability of our own dying, we cannot live fully.

Every death and grieving is an opportunity for deepening self-knowledge and love. When the veils between everyday material reality, and the mysteries of consciousness, soul and cosmos, become thin, then we are invited to step beyond, to see more and know more, to remember our place in the bigger harmony of life. Expanded and humbled, we are renewed.

Relationships Don't End at Death

Grieving for a loved one opens the possibility to heal the self and the relationship, even after the other is dead. I have come to know my brother, and to recognize his importance in my life, more after his death than I did in life. This realization brought loss closer and became a catalyst for deep healing, lightening my inner load and making more space for consciousness and creativity. I imagined my healing thoughts and emotions communicating with David's consciousness after he departed and bringing him comfort and release too.

Seven years after David's death he visits me often. Memories come unbidden and I still miss him. The loss hasn't gone away but I have learned to live with it and integrate it into my being. You could say my brother lives with me now in a way he didn't when he was alive. In life we were separated and now we are One. His physical absence exists side by side with this inner knowing that he is now part of me. Loss finds its place alongside gifts and gratitude.

Forgiveness, Compassion and Service

My journey has shown me that conscious healing involves a courageous pilgrimage into the darkness of human nature so that we may shine a light into the dark and redeem the power that has been repressed and hidden. By reflecting on my brother's life I came to a deeper understanding of how tenacious the roots of oppression are in human life and it was David's death that enabled me to more fully understand just how much we have all been distorted by history and conditioning. This finally enabled me to find forgiveness for my father and I see this as one of my biggest achievements. As a child, I saw with my own eyes, and felt in my own being, how my father passed on his frustrations and toxic shame to his family. As an adult, as I've reflected on what I know of his earlier life, the conditions in which he was raised and in which his parents and grandparents lived, and on and on back through history, my fear of him has softened to compassion.

When I look out at what is happening in the world today and see the majority of people on Earth are living in conditions barely fit to sustain human life, my heart breaks at the terrible waste of it all. Compassion for my family has deepened my compassion for the human condition and drawn me into belonging with the human family. As my understanding of the human journey towards liberation evolves I am less resistant and more available to serve life. This is an expansion of consciousness.

Befriending the Shadow

When we open our hearts and invite suffering to come in and share our hearth, then the darkness within us becomes less threatening and the heart softens into forgiveness. We recognise darkness is as much a part of who we are as the light, that we live on a revolving planet where darkness and light are equal partners in life.

One of the gifts of my conscious healing journey has been that I have stopped seeing my role as the family healer as a burden and begun to see it simply as who I am and why I am here. During this last transition into my fourth soul chapter, I've stopped resisting and feeling victimised by circumstances and instead I can better appreciate the abundant richness of life. I sometimes think those of us who live privileged lives in relatively peaceful locations often don't allow ourselves to fully take in and appreciate our blessings. We are aware of all the suffering and deprivation in the world and we can't really allow ourselves to have what we have been given. This applies to fully experiencing our sorrow too. And yet, until we fully own our gifts *and* our sorrows, we are keeping ourselves smaller than we could be. We are disempowering ourselves – and who does this serve?

Finding compassion for my father and releasing myself from the story of traumatic and toxic relationship, has allowed me to feel my sorrow more fully. By entering more deeply into my own shadow, I've come to a deeper appreciation of the wounds I've sustained and how these have been sources both of motivation and of suffering. I can no longer rationalise the sorrow or send it away; it is part of who I am. Perhaps, we never integrate our shadow but we learn how to befriend it, to walk alongside it and draw on its strengths.

Our social world is so polarised. We have been encouraged to pursue the light to the exclusion of the darkness. Whether our quest has been for spiritual enlightenment or more worldly achievements, we have been persuaded to chase personal success. And in this pursuit we have shunned and been ashamed of our suffering and hidden our failures. This only serves to intensify the darkness in which we all live.

When we turn to look into those parts of us that haven't seen the light for a long time and we become curious about what lies hidden there, we have the opportunity to open the door to our suffering and invite it in a little closer. And when we open our hearts and invite suffering to come in and share our hearth, then the darkness within us becomes less threatening and the heart softens into forgiveness. We recognise that the darkness is as much a part of who we are as the light, that we live on a revolving planet where darkness and light are equal partners in life. By bringing the love and wisdom of the soul into our daily lives we can become a bridge between the spacious, infinite possibility of Cosmos and the density of Earth; we can bring spirit into form.

Through this process of acceptance, inclusion and forgiveness, the self matures, expands and becomes more generous. And we know ourselves to be creative participants in a meaningful, evolving, conscious universal process. This is conscious evolution.

You Are Never Alone

At times this lifelong journey towards liberation is lonely. Many times I have felt like the only one out there on the edge of consciousness peering into the unknown for clues. But we are never alone. There are multitudes who have gone before us through the centuries of human history – pilgrims, visionaries, poets, change agents, healers, scientists, ordinary people living the best lives they could, led by a trust in something more and a longing to make a contribution. Those of us who are here now are walking in the footsteps of our ancestors, side by side, linking arms to encircle the world, carrying our gifts. There are many of us all around the world of all ages, races, walks of life and colours of skin and many more to come behind us, the children of the seven generations, born awake and walking more easily along the tracks we have trodden.

You are never alone because you always have access to sources of deeper wisdom and higher inspiration. Your soul is always guiding you; your inner light shines even in the deepest darkness. The species Soul, the evolutionary impulse, the wisdom of the Earth, the emerging collective consciousness, are here to guide, inspire and comfort you too.

All you have to do is pause, be present, connect and listen.

Practice: Connecting

Join me now. Pause and take a breath. Feel the sensation of air entering your nasal passage and the movement of your body as it expands in response. Air is the breath of life and it connects you with everything and everyone. Feel the touch of air on your skin...

Imagine a warm sunny day when the air is rich with the scent of flowers.

Imagine a crisp winter day when the chilly air makes the skin of your face taut.

Imagine light raindrops rolling down your cheeks.

Now bring your awareness into your feet as they make contact with the floor. Experience the contact between the sole and heel of your foot and the solidity of the floor. Imagine you are standing barefoot on the earth and your feet are putting down roots. Feel the earth solid, alive and breathing beneath you.

Feel the sensations of walking on damp grass ... on a sandy beach... up a rocky mountain ... through a beautiful park full of bright flowers and shrubs.

Visualise all the tiny creatures living beneath the earth and close to the earth – the worms, the bugs, the pollinators. Allow your imagination to spread out to touch all the animals who share your neighbourhood - the beloved domestic pets: the cats and dogs and horses; the farm animals: the sheep, the cows, goats, pigs, hens, ducks. And all the wild animals: the foxes, badgers, ferrets and stoats, mice and voles and rats. And the birds: magpie, pigeon, dove, sparrow, robin, hawk.

You are not alone. Even our nature-depleted world is teeming with life, now, in this moment, all around you. Imagine how much more life there will be when we humans make more space for nature and nurture it in all its forms.

You are part of the movement of life and evolving consciousness. All you need to do is pause and take a moment to remember and connect.

This awakening from the illusion of separation is our liberation. The freedom I am finding is gentler than anything I had imagined – it is here, now, in the smallest things, in each choice to connect and be open-hearted, in every act of kindness.

Perhaps choosing life as a daily practice is as simple as this.

Gratitude and Generosity

However it comes, death invites us into a greater intimacy with the darker, shadow side of human nature – our own and that of our species. If we do not shy away, we may open more fully to the hidden gifts and unknown mysteries of being human.

On my spiritual quest I have been blessed with awakened experiences, free from suffering, and I have also learned not to become too attached to them or identified with them. Enlightenment does not mean living exclusively in ecstasy. We are spiritual beings here on Earth to experience all it means to be human and then to uplift that experience. Grief and suffering are woven through our human lives along with beauty, love and joy. It is all part of the package, the gift of life.

When you make the conscious choice to stay open, life flows in and you fully experience it, here, now, this. And, as you receive all that is here, the heart fills with gratitude and a natural stream of generosity spills out from you. You find your belonging within a continual natural process of receiving and giving back.

Even now, amidst all the turmoil of the world, life is abundantly generous. You reach an understanding that even those parts of your life story you've wanted to deny or avoid are full of gifts. Even suffering is a gift. All of life is here to show you who you really are. Your shadow can become a source of strength when you befriend it and walk alongside it.

Inter-being

In the act of sitting with death, we may discover our ability to deepen our love, understanding and compassion for what it is to be alive on a sentient planet. Then we can expand our possibilities as we consciously choose to be creative participants in the magic and mystery of life.

My brother's death, and my reflections on his life, have reminded me of my quest to understand and live a journey of liberation. As a child I knew there was something more; as a young adult I discovered my connection with soul and found meaning and passion through pursuing my soul work; at mid-life I was guided by soul to quest for spiritual freedom; now, in the fourth chapter of my soul journey, the story I am interested in is that of inter-being. This was a term first coined by Thich Nhat Hahn, Buddhist monk, teacher and author,[3] and named by Deep Ecologist, Joanna Macy, as "dependent co-arising" or "the radical inter-dependence of all phenomena."[4] It is the realisation that all of life is one inter-woven whole and there can be no individual liberation until all are free. Each of us is a cell in the body of humanity and a cell in the body of life. The more we become healthy life-giving cells, the more we entrain and uplift other cells. It is this practice of becoming a healthy life-giving cell in the body of humanity, that I call Choosing Life.

We are not alone but part of a movement of evolving consciousness. Awakening from the illusion of separation is our liberation. The freedom I am finding is not a licence to do as I please and go where I want but the freedom to be of service to the greater Whole of life by realising and expressing my authentic self. I can think of no greater privilege than this.

It is Possible to Live a Fulfilled Life Within a World in Chaos

Not only is it possible to be fulfilled, I believe it is the responsibility for those of us who live in privileged and more peaceful worlds to act from a state of fulfilment rather than from a sense of lack. This might seem contradictory since I have gone to some length to persuade you to enter into your losses but it is only by attending to our losses that we can find our wholeness. And it is only in the quest for wholeness that you will find your gifts and be persuaded to take the risk of offering them.

I consider myself hugely privileged to live in an area of outstanding natural beauty and peace. To my younger adventure-seeking self the tranquillity and lack of distraction I now enjoy would have seemed stultifying. It has been the focus of my most recent transition into elderhood to surrender to and accept this quietude which gives me the ideal environment in which to write and complete my soul mission.

As I complete a soul chapter and my seven years of grief, I bring the gifts of **healing and integration.**

From the wellspring comes **the renewal of meaning and purpose.**

From the letting go of judgment and shame, **a new spaciousness; a rekindled appetite for life and the sensing of new possibilities.**

From the suspension of beliefs and the willingness to embrace uncertainty arise **revitalised curiosity and a desire to go on exploring, discovering and pushing back the edges of consciousness.**

From the courage to face into aloneness, comes a **re-energised commitment to participate in co-creating a future which will honour life in all its forms, and to do this in my own unique way, as part of the bigger conversation with life.**

In the course of this I am developing some new skills:

Allowing, Witnessing and Receiving

> *To move forward with grace, we need only align with what is true in ourselves, trust the natural unfolding of the bigger life of which we are each a part, listen deeply to life's intelligence and co-operate skilfully with it.*

The act of grieving opens the heart and transforms pain and heaviness by unlocking our innate love and wisdom. This can lead to the shift from 'efforting' and pursuing time-limited goals to allowing, witnessing, receiving and facilitating the emergence of new possibilities unfolding at the edge of life. Some might call this a shift to a more Feminine, intuitive, natural way of being. It is the essential paradigm shift so many people are talking about now which enables us to live in harmony and co-operation with life so that we can individually and collectively give birth to the whole new human and a whole new world.

Receiving is an important skill to practise because no real change can happen until we fully receive our gifts and integrate them into our being. Many of us have spent a lifetime resisting and blocking real nourishment and so when we reverse this and become open to receive it changes everything.

Practice: The Art of Receiving

1. Develop Awareness

During the course of any ordinary day begin by noticing any ways you are closed to receiving good things. For example, someone pays you a simple compliment:

"I love your skirt/jumper/shirt." And you say, "oh, this old thing, I've had it for years".

Or they say, "You're looking great today" and you say "oh, what about the bags under my eyes?"

Or notice how, when you're outside, maybe going for a walk, your head is full of thoughts and things to do and you don't notice the beautiful day, the sun on your face, the colours of the flowers in the hedgerow.

If you are closed to receiving in these simple everyday ways then you will surely be closed in bigger ways – closed to the realization of your gifts, to inspiration, to encouragement, to abundance.

Notice without judgment and make new choices.

2. Practice: Being More Open

Next time someone pays you a compliment about anything, pause, take a deep breath and take the appreciation in, then simply say thank you.

Or, next time you are out for a walk consciously practice noticing the beauty that surrounds you. Again, breathe it in, allow it to enter your being and touch you and say thank you.

Notice how you feel when you really allow appreciation, love and beauty to touch you. Can you take this loving energy right into your body and let it fill your heart and belly? Or do you clench up and resist? Again, just notice, don't judge. Take a breath.

3. Start a Gratitude Practice

Every evening, before you go to bed, or in any quiet moment, remember all the gifts the day has brought you. Start with the easy, obvious gifts, such as a friend's smile or a breakthrough in your work.

Then reflect on a more difficult event, such as a disappointment or bad news and see if you can find a gift in that. You might try holding the disappointment in your heart and surrounding it with unconditional love. Breathe gratitude through your being.

More skills:

Embracing Paradox

> *One of the most obvious paradoxes for all of us at this moment*
> *is to hold the urgency of our collective plight in one hand and,*
> *while taking some necessary holding actions, to patiently unfold*
> *the deep process of transformation with the other hand.*

The Soul Journey presents us with many paradoxes which in turn reveal the relationship between our human and soul perspectives.

This deepening into the complexity and paradoxes of life is a gift of grief. Life is no longer black and white but beautiful in many shades. Polarities soften, judgments fade, the eyes become kinder. We deepen our trust in the intelligence of life and in the unfolding process.

Commitment Combined with Non-attachment

The skill of non-attachment is the opposite of being dissociated, numb, or uncaring. We need to care very much what happens to life on Earth so that we can mobilise ourselves to do our soul work and keep taking actions towards a healthy, sustainable society. At the same time it is important to remain unattached to the results of our actions. When we are attached we can become wilful, we think we know what is right, we may bludgeon others into adopting our ways, we strive and push and overwork, or we become disheartened and give up. The egoic mind wants to be the one who knows, the one who gets there first, wants to be seen as special and successful. Non-attachment arises from an open mind, a loving heart and a trust in a grander intelligence.

Beginner's Mind: The Ability to Be in the Unknown

This is not about "dumbing down" or pretending or permanently abandoning hard-won wisdom, it's about suspension of what you already know in order

to make room for new ideas and perspectives to emerge. A large part of what
makes it possible to live on the edge of evolution is to be in a state of perpetual
and profound receptivity. If we want to be available to the movements of
the Spirit, if we want to be able to change and discover new things, we have
to be willing to constantly let go of all our fixed ideas and look again.
Craig Hamilton[5]

Beginner's mind is another state I have come to love – the ability to be in the unknown without reaching for easy answers. Here is a description of beginner's mind I wrote in my book, Deep Discovery Conversations.[6]

"An inquiry is a quest. It starts with a question and the question calls us to open and deepen and expand into our most creative knowing. This is not a knowing that has a goal, an end point. Instead it is open ended, informed by an awareness that reality is limitless - there is always more to discover, always more to know and further to go into mystery.

To be in beginner's mind is to be aware of this limitless reality and to remember the bigger mystery in which we live. To enter this larger context, we put aside our roles, status and expertise; our need to be the one who knows, to be right and to make another wrong. We suspend all disbelief, become keenly aware of our resistances and our desire to argue; and let these go, so that we simply open to what is arising in this moment in the expanded co-created field. With these actions we strip ourselves of defences, becoming vulnerable and open-hearted. While this requires a certain kind of courage and risk-taking it is also a way of stepping through, and beyond, fear by allowing curiosity to take over.

When we step innocently, humbly, and oh so curiously, into the unknown, we open to the understanding that every voice carries a piece of a bigger truth and we become intensely curious about what each person has to say and what their words touch, spark and reveal in us.

Together we can weave a tapestry which, at the best of times, is a magic carpet transporting us into a more expanded sense of wholeness and possibility."

Equanimity

I love the experience of equanimity. That sense of balancing effortlessly at the still centre of the turning world is relaxing, without effort. It is closely aligned to non-attachment. I'm committed to those things I hold dear without being attached to the results. I'm focused and intentional and yet I have an open mind and an experimental mindset. Because I know I am part of an interconnected world and consciousness and I am never alone, I enter into creativity as play rather than as work or as a burden I have to carry. I still work hard and focus and I'm serious about what I want to achieve but I trust in a bigger process and timing. I do what I can and then leave the results to life.

Discernment

To enjoy equanimity I need to know when to apply effort and when to let go and trust. This involves a willingness to experiment and to accept that I won't always get the results I want. I try something and notice what happens, then I adjust and try something else. I pay attention and read the context I'm operating within. An example of this is when I'm offering a group experience around grief or leadership, or whatever it happens to be. Sometimes it all comes together effortlessly, at other times it doesn't. There can be many reasons why something I've set my heart on isn't happening. Do I need to be more skilful in how I make my offering? Is this not the best time? Do I really want to do it? Is this really my work to do? Discernment helps me to make informed guesses and to adapt accordingly.

Deep Listening

I have extolled the virtues of deep listening throughout this book and it is the key to unlocking the treasure trove of wisdom and love that is within us. Deep listening requires presence, awareness, intention and the suspension of egoic consciousness. It opens the way for endless conversations with Soul and unlimited inspiration and insight. It is a bridge between the inner and outer worlds; through deep listening I can hear what others are saying with empathy, curiosity and compassion. It also enables me to take care of myself, to know when I have done enough for now and need to stop and rest, when I need to draw a boundary, when I am in danger, or to discern what my next step might be.

Patience

This is another lovely skill which I have taken a lifetime to learn. I enjoyed my earlier restlessness and the thrill of adventure, now I am content to sit and listen to what is required, to move forward slowly, without rushing or pushing or getting stressed by the need for accomplishment. Patience opens an expanded sense of time and an ability to touch the eternity of the soul's cycles.

Letting Go

I discovered that what I thought was emptiness is actually a source of love, alive with possibilities and full of gifts.

Letting go can feel like one of the most risky parts of the transformational process, especially when it involves relinquishing the old identity and story and stepping into the unknown. Perhaps we are afraid of falling and we fear the act of letting go in case there is nothing there to catch us. However, when the effort of holding everything together becomes intolerable, surrender brings sweet relief.

It is in the willingness to shed inflexible and limiting ideas of who we are that the evolution of humanity lies. Over time, I've discovered that what I thought was emptiness is actually a source of love, alive with possibilities and full of gifts. In the act of sitting with death, we may discover our ability to deepen our love, our understanding and compassion for what it is to be human. We can expand our possibilities as we consciously choose to be creative participants in life.

Making Choices and Taking Actions

*When we commit to a path of conscious healing there are many ways
we send ripples through the collective. Grieving consciously can be a
gateway into a deep collective healing process that gives rise to a new
consciousness and a new culture in harmony with life. As we enlighten the
cells of our being we stimulate a new archetype for the transformation of
humanity. This is how consciousness grows and spreads – each individual
contribution changes the mind and heals the heart of humanity.*

While I was living alone on my hilltop in Wales, I deepened my understanding
of sacred activism when I realised that, even if nobody ever reads a word I've
written, just by virtue of the act of attention, intention, deep listening and
the energetic movement which is writing, I can bring thought forms from
the unseen worlds and release them into the collective consciousness. Since
we are each part of One Consciousness, people around the world in many
places receive similar inspirations and guidance simultaneously. By actively
engaging with this inspiration we integrate it into our experience in our
own unique way. As we bring an inspired, expanded intelligence through
the body our ideas ripple out to touch others who are ready to receive them.

As I've told you, my understanding of Soul, soul work and the Soul
Journey began when I started to write poetry in my late twenties. I came
to see myself as an archaeologist of soul, a woman patiently scraping at
the earth to uncover treasures. To others these may appear to be little
more than meaningless fragments but the fragments carry within them
the whole colourful mosaic, for eyes that wish to see. Through offering
courses and writing books I have done my best to pass on whatever skills
and understanding I am learning, and I've touched many people in this way.
But perhaps, it has been the inner work, the patient sitting with, suffering
with, and witnessing the death of the false self, that has been my most
valuable contribution. I know now, without a doubt, that individual choices
and actions can, and do, make a difference and contribute to the evolution
of human life on Earth. Realizing this is a great gift.

Further Realisations:

Resonance is the Call of Soul

Writing this book and creating the *Sitting with Death and Choosing Life Programme* have been big gifts of my conscious healing process. My ability to create something out of "nothing" is a privilege and a challenge that stretches me beyond my limits. But I have said before and I will say again, the work has a life of its own. I am in service to a bigger intelligence which guides and directs me. Soul sounds a note and that note sends a resonance vibrating within the body. As I hear that note I say yes over and over again, reconfirming my willingness and commitment. Those who have been drawn to work with me have responded to that same resonance and those who read this book will be feeling that resonance too. The more I can align my being with that note, the more clearly I broadcast the call of Soul and the more easily others can respond. As I've taken each step forward, the more the work has called me out. I am committed now to releasing this book into the world so that it can touch, inspire and heal others and this will stretch me further. I also know that, even if I do nothing more to further this work, the word is out, the transformation of consciousness is under way. I am one of a multitude of voices speaking the wisdom that is coming through us from many sources and expressing the truths that need to be spoken and heard at this time.

Home is Where Our Wholeness Lives

All of this has helped me to more deeply understand the myth of the Hero's Journey as told in the Arthurian legend of the Holy Grail in the 12th century. The hero, or in my case the heroine, leaves home and sets off on adventures which will test her and bring her self-knowledge and the knowledge of what it means to be human. Only after many trials does she earn the right to return home, healed and whole, and capable of healing others.

The conditions of my childhood, which appeared to be unfortunate, were the seedbed for everything that has given my life meaning, purpose and direction. The death of a family member is a wonderful opportunity to discover the gifts that lie within the grieving process. As I've grieved the loss of my brother, I've allowed grief to guide my growth and show me where I need to become more conscious, more caring, less selfish and more self-loving. And I have also learned that much of this grief is not personal at all, it is transpersonal, part of the human condition. I have followed the call to become an alchemist, transmuting grief for myself, for others, and for the web of life. When I'm sad I know now there isn't something wrong with me. Instead, I have come to see this grieving path, this process of descent into full humanness, which includes embracing death and shadow, is what my soul has chosen. Maybe we can only step onto the stairway to heaven when we've been right down to the bottom rung.

While every death and grieving is an opportunity for deepening self-knowledge and love, for those of us on a conscious healing path, a death is also an opportunity to co-operate with the process of growing and healing the soul. The thinning of the veils between everyday material reality and the mysteries of consciousness and cosmos beyond, is an invitation to step forward, to see more and know more, to remember our place in the bigger dance of life, to be both expanded and humbled, renewed and distilled to essence.

Each of Us is an Opening into the Transpersonal

We are so attached to our individuality, and yet, whenever I take the time and care to be with my own or another's story, I realise each of us is an opening into the transpersonal. Through grieving for my brother I came to appreciate, in a very personal and intimate way, just how much the human race has been oppressed and repressed throughout the ages and how this has affected our collective well-being, our creativity and our capacity to participate fully in a shared story. Feeling this keenly has enabled me to deepen my compassion for all beings and provided a major expansion of love and meaning. The work of grief is in allowing our humanity, in all its aspects, to move through us and to transform the heart. Feeling into my brother's losses brought me closer to him. I felt I was grieving *with* him and I imagined him burning off his old story and attachments as he passed into the next dimension of the spirit world lighter and freer. As I hold together the knowledge of human oppression throughout the ages with the recognition of the heroic journey towards freedom, I feel a deep settling within me of meaning, purpose and direction. I thank my brother for this.

There Can Be No Individual Liberation Until All Are Free

I have been drawn for a long time to the Bodhisattva vow and the idea that there can be no such thing as individual liberation or enlightenment until everyone is free and enlightened. This doesn't mean that individually we cannot become more peaceful, loving and harmonious. Indeed, it is our responsibility to be so. I believe, we in the West who live privileged lives in comparison to the majority of people on Earth, need to change our ideas of what freedom is. Freedom is an opportunity to serve and service is where we will find our fulfilment.

This prayer fell into my inbox the other day:

The Bodhisattva Prayer for Humanity

May I be a guard for those who need protection

A guide for those on the path

A boat, a raft, a bridge for those who wish to cross the flood

May I be a lamp in the darkness

A resting place for the weary

A healing medicine for all who are sick …

Until all beings are freed from sorrow

And all are awakened.

This prayer was written by Shantideva, a Buddhist monk of the Mahayana tradition who lived around 700 AD. He was a devoted practitioner who authored the Bodhicaryavatara or Bodhisattva Way of Life.[7]

Choose Life

What is life?

We live within a solar system on an outer spiral arm in the vast Milky Way galaxy within a universe comprised of billions of galaxies. The human mind cannot begin to comprehend the scope of this space in which our blue-green planet revolves. So far, no other planet that supports life has been discovered, let alone the diversity of species we enjoy on Earth, or the intricate genius of civilisations. In the face of such facts I can only conclude that life is special and precious. One need only watch any one of the wildlife documentaries created by David Attenborough[8] to be reminded how stunningly beautiful, intricate and fragile life is. Woods too was very sensitive to this:

> *The fact of being mysteriously and exquisitely alive is nearly more*
> *than a conscious human can withstand. I call the understandably*
> *disconcerted human response to a mysterious life and a dazzling cosmos,*
> DAZZLEPHRENIA. *It's no wonder we're all half mad from this alone.*
> *People stay nearly asleep and oblivious to their cosmic setting to protect*
> *themselves from being shaken to the core. But the heroic challenge is to try*
> *and take it all in, anyhow, for the hell of it, go for the whole of it, open up to*
> *it, become fully aghast and bedazzled. Pretending it's just an ordinary life*
> *is to minimize and downplay what an entirely extraordinary life we are.*[9]

Why is it so difficult for we humans to truly value life and give it the respect it needs to maintain integrity? Perhaps that is another way of saying why is it so difficult for you and me to truly value ourselves and give ourselves and each other the respect we need? I hope my explorations in this book have thrown a little light on the tensions in which we humans live – the tension between our desire to thrive and the entropy of old habits; the tension that exists between the guidance of our soul and the waywardness of our personality; between the pull towards individuality and self-interest and our longing to belong within the interconnected web of relationship that is life. Then throw into the mix the different levels of consciousness in which people live, the desperation caused by poverty and inequality and the gross distortions of thinking amongst some politicians and corporate magnates.

Put First Things First

But let's stay with what we can change and influence - our self - the starting place for change.

For me, choosing life is about putting first things first – knowing what I value and making that my priority. This becomes evident in the unfolding rhythm of my days.

These days, when I get out of bed I cross the hallway to my office, sit down at my desk, open up my computer and pick up once more the weaving of this book. This is a labour of love, an ongoing conversation with my soul. Ever since poems began to flow through my arm onto paper, being in conversation with soul has been my first priority, my primary relationship. Later in the day I will be a companion to my partner and our dog, I'll tend to the garden and walk on the beach, always grateful for the beauty that is here, I will talk with a friend or read a book, I'll cook tasty meals and watch a movie. But first I choose to sit here with my writing and listen for the meaning that is weaving through the form. As an archaeologist, I scrape gently at the earth to reveal what has been lost and forgotten. As a sculptor, I chip away at every word that is not essential attempting to bring forth the inner beauty. As a fisherwoman I cut my circle in the ice and wait.

Iceberg

1.

I could draw poetry out of silence

with the patience of a fisherwoman
I cut my circle in the ice

and wait.

2.

I want to find the courage
to dive deep beyond conception
and hammer diamonds from the glassy wall
I'll suck hard at meaning
and make transparent the opaque.

I want to trace with burning fingers
the unique and perfect pattern of each frost flower
to wear a skin so thin
my blood's heat will melt
the edge of ice
and make the inert flow.

3.

I want to write poetry with muscle
words that won't be pummelled into submission
but swagger seeking across a page.

I want a new vocabulary for living
a grammar for contradictions
where mind and body rhyme
and my heart's beat
sounds in the sea.

Rose Diamond[9]

The Quiet Patience of Crafting a Life

When I lived with Woods in Virginia, USA, I would often sit and watch him caning chairs. He had taken over the conservatory at the back of the house and made the big billiard table into his workbench. Canes of all sizes escaped from their spiral packaging across the table mingling with one another, while Woods stood at the head of the table with his latest chair. Some of the chairs were antiques, big and old, with intricate cane seats in need of repair.

The conservatory was surrounded on three sides with big windows through which we could see hummingbirds drinking nectar from the feeders and grey squirrels racing through the branches with manic acrobatic leaps. Woods listened to music as he worked – opera, classical, pop, new age, or the calm voice of Eckhart Tolle would draw me in to listen.

He had taught himself to be an artisan at midlife when he grew out of his life as a psychotherapist in New York and set off to begin anew in the mountains of Colorado. He perfected his craft by practicing a few hours every day. Steadfast and patient, there were times when he'd be very nearly at the end of his work on a chair when he noticed he'd made a mistake early on in the weave. He'd unpick right back to the mistake and begin again. He tried to encourage me to learn but I didn't have the patience for it.

Now my weaving of this book, *A Story of Transformation*, feels very similar. It is taking longer than I'd expected but the work can't be hurried. There have been several times when I thought I was nearly at the end and then I realised no, the meaning isn't yet clear, the beauty of the form isn't yet shining through, and I chose to go back and listen again, more deeply, reaping the quiet satisfaction of patience.

When this book began its life seven years ago, as my companion through the grief of my brother's death, I also created a garden of potted plants on the gravel courtyard in front of my cottage. The garden grew and grew because I love flowers and I couldn't resist bringing home new ones whenever I had the chance. The joy of a container garden is the freedom to move the pots around and make the colour combinations, textures and forms more harmonious and striking. I moved my pots around frequently. And yet, after a few years, I longed to be able to plant those flowers and salad greens into the earth, to give them room to spread and follow their own ways. And so, when I began a new relationship and my partner offered me his back garden to play in, I jumped at the opportunity. A year later I took up my pots from the cottage and came to live with him and the garden. Those roots were so happy to be released into the earth where they could spread through the mycelium. Some of the plants survived and thrived, some were gobbled up by slugs, others simply faded away and disappeared. My job as a novice gardener was to notice, to provide compost and water, remove the choking weeds, add a bit of colour here, a bit of space there.

This book has had a similar evolution. I completed the first draft as best I could in my first labour of grief. Every book starts as a conversation with oneself, but it is also a bigger conversation trying to find expression and needs readers to complete it, and so I put the book to work as a means to attract others to come and explore with me. My inquiry into these shared human experiences of loss, grief, death, healing, the dark nights of the soul, is a living inquiry with a life of its own, a life that I've tended through my inner conversations with soul and through conversations with others. As the inquiry grew into an educational programme and took off on its own trajectory, at times, I have to admit, it has all felt too much. This attempt to find words for the raw emotions of grief and loss, this baring of my soul on subjects that most people keep quiet and private, this calling to go deeper and further, has all felt too impossibly much.

And yet here I am, very close to the completion of the book and now, in these final weeks it has become an integration, a synthesis not only of my seven years of grief but of my whole life. Although in one sense it will never be complete because there is always more to discover and I will never be fully satisfied with what I have achieved, as I come near to the end I am at peace with this book of my life. Soon I will have done enough and I'll sign off with the last full stop and step away from the computer screen. Then I'll release this conversation with my soul into the world to do its work and find its way.

I am ready for another soul chapter, a new book perhaps. Through conscious acts of grieving and the integration of the gifts of grief, I have opened the way to choose life more fully.

What Does it Mean to Choose Life?

In this final passage, let's have a conversation about what choosing life might be.

For me, choosing life means saying YES wholeheartedly to life. Every day.

It means being willing to embrace all aspects of being human – the dark as well as the light; peace and contentment as well as heartbreak and anger. I choose to allow, contain and listen to it all.

Choosing life is about allowing the flow of life, inviting life to flow through me, change me and put me to work. It's about choosing to do no harm, to leave the lightest footprint on the Earth, to spread love rather than fear, to respect and nurture all beings and life forms.

And it's about deeply listening to my soul and taking the risks necessary to fulfil my soul contracts and purpose.

One thing I'm sure about is that none of us can fully choose life unless we are also willing to sit with death. When a loved one dies, or we receive a worrying health diagnosis, or a catastrophe happens on our doorstep, we are brought face to face with our own inevitable death. We remember that we too will die and we don't know when. We realise life is precious and this can lead to soul-searching about what we really want to do with the days and years we have left and who we want to be in response to all that is arising in our world.

It seems to me this choice for fully lived life is one we face every day: am I committed to living fully or do I rather choose to deaden and compromise myself? Certainly, when we are grieving or impacted by so much suffering in our world, the choice for life becomes harder as well as more urgent. But when we turn our back on grief, or we don't know how to complete it, the flow of life becomes blocked and we are no longer able to participate and contribute fully.

Life is a constant flow of energy, information and inspiration. Life is abundant, generous and ingenious. It is a process of constant change. Life can also be destructive, disruptive, full of paradox and uncertainty. To choose life is to say yes to all of this.

These are my questions for inquiry today:

What does it take to choose life?

How do you feel, and how do you act, when you're fully committed to living?

What is a healthy and responsible self-love?

If you were sure the choices you make really do affect humanity's evolution, as well as your own well-being, would you live differently?

Would you be a little more courageous, a little less ambivalent?

Living in a global culture of accelerating fragmentation, polarisation and alienation, as we do, it is a big challenge for any of us to maintain the expanded state of consciousness which is essential for living a fulfilled life and bringing about positive change. The art of living in a world that is so much in distress, while fulfilling our destiny as souls, is an ongoing discipline, yet, to my mind, the soul journey is the best adventure life can offer.

When we are overwhelmed by bad news, or shaken by shock, our awareness contracts and we can easily become disconnected from self, others, nature and the web of life. A typical response to the pain of disconnection is to lose ourselves in the distraction of social media, in driven busy-ness, emotional numbing, spiritual by-passing or isolation. This is not new but the disconnection and contraction has intensified in the years since the COVID pandemic. Similar to the trauma I experienced in response to my father's rageful behaviour, the breakdown of national and global ecosystems causes a contraction in our being and this inevitably means we no longer have all our mental, emotional, spiritual and creative powers available to us. As a consequence, we can easily lose confidence in our gifts and the will to act, which in turn robs us of our innate sense of meaning, purpose and direction. A participant in one of my groups described this as a "massive contraction" leading to "loss of engagement". At a time when humanity and the world desperately needs each of us to show up with creative solutions to our common problems, so many of us are becoming more isolated, creatively diminished and cut off from our authentic wisdom.

A simple yet radical alternative to this trajectory towards diminishing personal power is to turn and face into the many losses and deaths that happen in a lifetime, both personal and collective. We can choose to see and to accept them as natural and inevitable aspects of life. Emotional discomfort, rather than something to avoid, is an opportunity to become more conscious and to heal. When we give ourselves space to feel our pain, our suffering and discontent, we can release limiting patterns of thought and behaviour associated with our grief. Then we can discover the gifts within the grief and integrate these into our being. This releases any stuck creative energy that has been held in the body and the mind and, as we become lighter and more expanded, a natural movement emerges. We become stronger, more resilient and more available to participate creatively in life.

This is what I call choosing life.

To turn towards our pain in this way is not easy; it takes courage and skill. Personal and collective healing requires time and space and we go against cultural conditioning when we choose to sit with our suffering. Our world desperately needs a new consciousness that honours being as well as doing; that recognises human shadow and darkness as well as human genius and joy; that embraces failure as well as success; that values wisdom, intuition, and vision as well as focus, achievement and accountability. None of us can make this radical shift alone. We need the support of each other within intentional spaces where we can create islands of coherence within the collective sea of chaos which dominates our world today.

Practice: Choosing Life

It is possible to manage, and even to transform, our inner conflicts and tendencies towards entropy but it requires a concerted, committed effort; a belief in something bigger that gives meaning and purpose; simple practices repeated daily;

support and immersion in a loving energy field. It is this transformational possibility which I have been exploring through this book and these are the skills and practices I have recommended to you:

1. **Clearly identify your big picture philosophy,** or what some people call your BIG WHY, your reason for being here, the way that you make sense of life and find meaning and purpose. Completing a Life Review will help you with this.

2. **Identify your questions and live your questions as an inquiry,** as a conversation with soul and with life.

3. **Clarify your values** – what qualities are the most important for you to develop and embody in this lifetime?

4. Are you ready to commit to living and embodying these values? If you are ready, then **set a clear intention** and keep that intention in mind every day.

5. Then follow your intention with **daily choices.** For example, if the value you wish to develop and embody is authenticity choose every day to express yourself truly. Notice when you fall short and use that as an opening for healing.

6. Do all the necessary inner work to become aware of and to **integrate your shadow.**

7. Back up your choices with **practices.** Use some of the practices offered here – the practice for transforming reactivity into acceptance on page 11. Or the practice for connecting, on page 152

8. **Find your favourite vehicles for transformation** – whether it is writing, dance, art, being an entrepreneur, an environmental activist – whatever it is that's written in your heart, do it, enjoy it, grow with it, let it stretch you.

9. Take **consistent experimental actions** – focused and intentional but without attachment to ideas of success or failure.

10. **Seek out soul friends and like-minded tribes** with whom you can explore all of this through conversations.

There are certain authors and sub-cultures within the world of personal and spiritual development who claim that, with the right attitude, everything will be easy and, if not, you must be doing something wrong. That has not been my experience. It is easy to say the words "transformation" and "renewal", but it takes courage and resilience to face the dying away of everything you have held dear and true, with no guarantee the new will be born. This is a place many of us visit after losing a loved one and it is also part of our collective reality now when so much is being destroyed in our world. The heartbreak is unbearable at times. And yet, when the grieving is happening and I am in it, I simply have to go with it and trust.

Choice dawns slowly, and slowly intention gathers, and with intention comes the decision to trust, even when there seems to be nothing left to trust in. From the tilled earth of endurance, patience and surrender, and the willingness to sit with emptiness, tendrils of new life begin to reach out. From this act of holding firm and still amidst a tempest of deep and often conflicting feeling, the miracle of transformation arises, and the stream of life lifts and carries us gently into our next more loving and free expression.

A choice for fully lived life doesn't just happen. It is a decision to be made and then a nurtured every day. And the choice for me is:

If I am to have another chapter of life, possibly my last chapter, how can I create a quality of life to carry me into older age, and towards death, in a way that is honouring of myself and my brother, and of the best of what it means to be human?

How may I live with grace?

And what is left for me to do?

Rose Diamond

All the words that slip so easily from the tongue yet are so elusive in everyday life: peace, beauty, love, harmony, justice, freedom, meaning, unity, compassion, community, service – these are words that inspire me. This is what I choose. I choose to walk with my shadow and to be guided by my soul, and to live in grace, love and freedom.

Aho. And so it is.

Conclusion
In Our Ending is Our Next Beginning

I hope my story has touched you and caused you to reflect on your own and to become a little clearer in response to the questions of life and death that live inside you. This is in an extraordinarily challenging turning point in our history when life itself is under threat as a consequence of human decisions and actions. And yet, at the heart of this book is a vision for a renewed humanity and an invitation to open our hearts a little more and to draw more light into this project of learning how to be fully human within an interconnected, soulful world.

The world we live in now has been fashioned from a partial view of what it means to be human. It is a world that has been stripped of the sacred and in which we have been trained to forget our connection with life and with soul. This old-world view has reached the end of its usefulness and is dying.

It is time to sit with death, to witness death, and to grieve. This is a big undertaking.

The outcome of our collective crises will be decided by just how skilful and resourceful each of us can be – individually and together. Our ability to face the death of the old; to release limiting beliefs and learn to live for a while empty; to break through the resistance of habits and unhealthy dependencies and enter new territory; to welcome the unknown; to transmute our grief into wisdom and our losses into gifts; and to enter a new more inclusive stage of consciousness – all of this will make the difference between whether we go down with the sinking ship of outworn dogma and a dysfunctional civilisation, and perish, or we live on as full participants in a new consciously co-created story.

The crises in our world point to a collective movement through death to possible new life and the process of transformation is happening now. My invitation to you through this book is to choose to connect with life every day and to become the channel through which soul can return to our world.

If this seems like a big daunting task, it is. But you don't have to try and change the whole world. You simply start where you are – with your own healing and wholing; with healing in the family; by bringing love, kindness and compassion into all your relationships; by creating conscious communities; by willingly playing your part and doing the work that has your name on it.

Twenty years ago I developed a project called A Whole New World. I was so excited by all the possibilities I could talk of nothing else. The people I lived amongst shared similar certainties that the crumbling of the old world would be followed by something so much better. We could feel it coming and it was just a matter of time. But in the last few years a collective dark night of the soul has drawn us into deep reflection and reassessment.

I don't want to sow seeds of false hope. I'm a baby boomer, born into a time of possibility after the ending of the Second World War, when England, the country where I was born, exploded with creativity and affluence. Much of that affluence was based on exploitation and has had tragic results. As I have shown through my own story, learning how to co-operate with the creative process is a long-term endeavour. Over the decades of my life it has become heartbreakingly clear just how challenging the transformation of consciousness is, how long it takes and the magnitude of the task. I only have to listen to the news on any ordinary day to remember how uncivilised we humans are. We are barely at the beginning of knowing how to live together in peace, harmony, respect for life and love. However, amidst the rampant greed, self-interest, inequality and violence of this era, I have met many good people and witnessed a new soulful consciousness arising and I have faith in the evolution of consciousness. I have taken a step back and looked at human history from the bigger perspective of Life on Earth, and I've come to the conclusion that the Whole New World is unlikely to happen in my lifetime. But even so, every step towards a new culture of peace and unity on Earth counts. We are part of the One consciousness, in a Cosmos that doesn't live by human time. Nothing is wasted, the whole unfolds to its own natural rhythm. Every conscious choice makes a difference.

This book is as much about choosing life, as it is about grief; as much about creative freedom, as it is about death. The process of transformation which I have described by telling my brother's story and my own, is simple but not easy. The new inclusive consciousness of Whole Mind-Whole World arises effortlessly when we are fully present, connected, embodied and open hearted. Then love, unity and interconnectedness — the foundations for a new culture of peace on our planet - become our natural way of being. You and I are powerful creators in training and we can make conscious choices every day. When you have sat with death you can choose what to bring into your newly emptied space.

What will you choose? Who will you choose to be?
Are you ready to create a whole new world?
Can you believe in that possibility? Can you envision it?

Imagine a new culture in which all individuals feel connected to a bigger shared purpose and free to live from their own truth and to offer their true gifts?

What one action can you take today towards that vision?

On the soul's journey, each lifetime is a new book and within a lifetime there are many chapters. We pass in and out of life and death like a needle weaving cloth. We gather chapters like beads strung on the web of time - the mala on the wrist of the Buddhist monk, the rosary beads of the catholic nun - counting, counting, counting. A big bead for a lifetime, three or four little beads for the chapters within a lifetime, a different sort of bead for the afterlife. Perhaps, the beads mark the doorways between transitions. How many doorways do we pass through before we reach a place where all beings are free from sorrow? Where all life is respected and nurtured? Where peace and harmony prevail? This possibility lives within the collective consciousness.

Can you imagine it?

Can we call it in and create it, here, now, where we live?

If you truly knew in your heart that you are the force for positive change our Earth and the Universe are longing for, and that perhaps the most vitally important thing you can do is to come to peace with your own experience of being human, what might you be moved to express or do?

Thank you for being here. There are millions of us on this journey of becoming more conscious and empowered. All around the world, we are of many races and colours, of all ages, genders and sexual orientations. Just pause a moment and imagine this great circle of people surrounding the planet, holding all life in unconditional love. All our loved ones who have passed over into death are here too cheering us on. Imagine the combined spiritual power of generations of people who have walked their own soul journey to uncover the riches within the treasury of Soul.

Perhaps, just perhaps, we can love our beautiful Planet Earth and all beings into its next renewed stage of life and consciousness.

I leave you with this prayer.

Invocation
Calling the Whole New Human

If your intention is to speak the wisdom that's aching to live through you

to warm the seed of peace with your trust

and water the seed of love with your truth

If you long with all your heart to be whole

to heal the cracks in the fractured mirror

and become one vibrant cell in a body of light encircling the world

If you'll carry the torch of awakening to the hills and valleys and mountains

We are of One Heart and I will stand by you.

Look to the person to your right and you will find me

Look to the person to your left, I am there too

Look within and know I am the One Heart beating

I am the sound of the drum calling the tribe.

Simply follow the path of gold across the water

keep walking into the aura of the moon

deeper and deeper, trusting and surrendering.

Take the next step for humanity now

and let the first act of a whole new story unfold.

Imagine, all over the world at this moment, people are
rousing, stretching, opening to celebrate each new day.

Imagine all personal dramas dropping away, leaving a clear space
in which we can feel, hear, touch and enjoy each other.

Imagine, life is a creative adventure and we are
stars spread out across an infinite sky

Millions of us, flowing in a wide river of light, winking back at the Milky Way.

And the Moon sings "Welcome home!

Pull your canoe up the shore to the wharenui

we have a place for you to stand tall

a safe place to voice your love and passion

a place where you can see the full scope of your vision.

Welcome, welcome home!

And we sing back to the Moon

Te Aroha, Te Whakapono,

Me te Rangimarie, Tatou Tatou e

Love, Trust, Peace, unite us.

Rose Diamond, from *Songs of Awakening*[10]

Rose Diamond
January 2024

Thank you David!

Next Steps

If my words have touched you and you have enjoyed participating in the inquiry and practices you may want to explore further with me. Alongside our stories, conversations are a powerful and exciting vehicle for collective growth. The honest and open sharing of our experience in conversations can help to move us all forward beyond loss and into new possibilities. I invite you to meet me in a space of inquiry and exploration so that we may learn, grow and evolve together and find fulfilment through following our soul's calling.

First, don't forget to get the free resources I have made to support you with the practices: https://www.tribeintransition.net/a-story-of-transformation-free-resources/

For all information about the **Sitting with Death and Choosing Life Programme.** Please take a look here: https://sittingwithdeathandchoosinglife.com/

Sign up for our newsletter on the home page to receive regular updates about taster workshops, deep discovery conversation circles, writing circles, courses, blog articles, new books and resources.

Or go to **Tribe in Transition,** www.tribeintransition.net to find out about community membership, coaching (including help with your Life Review) and more resources.

Join the **Tribe in Transition Community** on Facebook: https://www.facebook.com/groups/TribeinTransitionCommunity

Or find me on my blog: https://diamondr.substack.com/

References

Prelude

1 *Portrait of a Gentle Man - Soulful Living, Conscious Dying,* Rose Diamond 2016
2 *Deep Discovery Conversations – Awakening Community Wisdom for a New Era,* Rose Diamond, 2016
3 *The Sitting with Death and Choosing Life Programme,* https://sittingwithdeathandchoosinglife.com

How to Get the Best from this Book

1 *Letters to a Young Poet,* Rainer Maria Rilke, 1929, Penguin Random House UK, 2016
2 *Conscious Evolution: Awakening Our Social Potential,* Barbara Marx Hubbard, New World Library, 2015
3 *Evolutionary Enlightenment, A New Path to Spiritual Awakening,* Andrew Cohen, Select Books Inc, 2011
4 Image ©cloverlittleworld viaCanva.com
5 Image ©tannikart viaCanva.com

Chapter One: Grieving

1 *Little Wing,* Jimi Hendrix, Jimi Hendrix
https://www.youtube.com/watch?v=PJ-2XFQLZE8
2 *Eric Clapton, Eric Clapton, The Autobiography,* Century, 2007
3 *The House of the Lord,* John McLaughlin and Carlos Santana, https://www.youtube.com/watch?v=IB_F_vpl5bw
4 *Over the Rainbow,* Eric Clapton, Songwriters: Harold Arlen / E.y. Harburg
https://www.youtube.com/watch?v=PSelmsGeoPc

5   *Elegy to My Father*, Rose Diamond, 2011
6   *New and Selected Poems, Vol 1*, Mary Oliver Beacon Press, Boston, 1992
7   *The Prophet*, Kahlil Gibran, William Heinemann/Pan books, 1980
8   *The Sitting with Death and Choosing Life Programme*, https://sittingwithdeathandchoosinglife.com/
9   *The Sitting with Death and Choosing Life Conversations*, https://sittingwithdeathand choosinglife.com/swd-conversations/
10 *The Guest House*, Jellaludin Rumi, translation by Coleman Barks, Published in A Year with Rumi, HarperOne, November 2006
11 *For Memory*, Adrienne Rich, from *A Wild Patience Has Taken Me This Far*, Norton 1981
12 *He Aint Heavy, He's My Brother*, The Hollies, Songwriters: Bob Russell / Bobby Scott. https://www.youtube.com/watch?v=fBI9i3HlFVE

Chapter Three: Soul Work

1   *Migration to the Heartland, A Soul Journey in the Land of the Awakening Dawn*, Rose Diamond, 2005
2   *Four Quartets*, T.S.Eliot, Faber 1941
3   *The Divided Self, An Existential Study in Sanity and Madness*, R.D.Laing, Penguin Books 1967
4   *The Making of a Counter Culture*, Reflections on the Technocratic Society and Its Youthful Opposition, Theodore Roszak, Faber and Faber 1971
5   *Sexual Politics*, Kate Millett, Doubleday, 1971
6   *The Aquarian Conspiracy, Personal and Social Transformation in Our Time*, Marilyn Ferguson, Jeremy P. Tarcher, 1980
7   *Spiritual Emergency, When Personal Transformation Becomes a Crisis*, Stan Grof, Penguin, 1989
8   *A Wild Patience Has Taken Me This Far*, Adrienne Rich, Norton, 1981
9   *Migration to the Heartland, A Soul Journey in the Land of the Awakening Dawn*, Rose Diamond, 2005.
10 *Ibid*
11 *Living Your Passion, How Love-in-action is Seeding a Whole New World*, Roes Diamond, 2008
12 *Ram Dass*, for example, *Still Here – Embracing Aging, Changing and Dying*, Riverhead Books, 2001
13 *Song of Waitaha, Histories of a Nation*, Barry Brailsford, Waitaha Books,1994
14 *Little Gidding, Four Quartet*, T.S. Eliot, Faber 1941

15   *The Present Moment in Psychotherapy and Everyday Life*, Stern D (2004) quoted in Kalsched D *Trauma and the Soul*, Routledge, 2013
16   *Portrait of a Gentle Man*, Rose Diamond, 2016
17   *The Sitting with Death and Choosing Life Programme*
18   *Re-membering all the lost worlds*, Rose Diamond, 2022
19   *Whole Mind Whole World, The Power of Wise Choices, Creating a Future that Works for All*, Rose Diamond, 2019

Chapter Four: Existential Crisis and Transpersonal Grief

1   *Migration to the Heartland, A Soul Journey in the Land of the Awakening Dawn*, Rose Diamond, 2005.
2   *Whole Mind Whole World, The Power of Wise Choices, Creating a Future that Works for All*, Rose Diamond, 2019
3   *The Next Transition: The Evolution of Humanity's Role in the Universe*, Mary Evelyn Tucker and Brian Thomas Swimme, from *Spiritual Ecology, the Cry of the Earth*, Llewellyn Vaughan Lee, The Golden Sufi Center Publishing, 2013
4   Alexandra Derwen, https://www.derwenroots.wales/
5   Gloria Ogunbadejo, https://gloriaogunbadejo.com/
6   Jos Hadfield, https://www.roselidden.co.uk/about-us/
7   The Sitting with Death and Choosing Life Conversations Volume 4: Grieving for Our World. *https://sittingwithdeathandchoosinglife.com/swd-conversations/*

Chapter Five: Sitting with Death

1   *To Know the Dark, The Peace of Wild Things*, Wendell Berry, Random House 1964
2   William Meader, https://meader.org/
3   *Let Go*, from *Songs of Awakening*, Rose Diamond, 2012
4   *The Great Re-Cycling*, from *Songs of Awakening*, Rose Diamond, 2012

Chapter Six: Transformation

1   *The Sitting with Death and Choosing Life Programme* comprises five inter-related programmes:
     The Foundation Course,
     https://sittingwithdeathandchoosinglife.com/swd-foundation-course-web/
     The *Essential Skills for Grieving Well*,

https://sittingwithdeathandchoosinglife.com/web-the-essential-skills-for-grieving-well/
Deep Discovery Conversations,
https://sittingwithdeathandchoosinglife.com/web-deep-discovery/
The Facilitator Training,
https://sittingwithdeathandchoosinglife.com/web-facilitator-training/ a
Write Your Way Through Grief,
https://sittingwithdeathandchoosinglife.com/web-write-your-way-through-grief/
2 *The Emergence Foundation,* https://emergencefoundation.org/ a UK-based educational charity and grant-giving organisation which has offered financial support to individual and group projects and initiatives that are engaged in and committed to the uplift of individuals, organisations and culture at large: projects that affect a shift in consciousness and perspective based on the fundamental unity of all life, providing a force of positive change in the world.
3 *Deep Discovery Conversations,* see above.
4 *Extinction Rebellion,* https://extinctionrebellion.uk
5 *Death Café,* https://deathcafe.com/

Chapter Seven: Choosing Life

1 *Your Soul Basket,* Rose Diamond, 2012, from Songs of Awakening
2 *East Coker, from Four Quartets,* T S Eliot, Faber 1941
3 *Thich Nhat Hahn,* see https://www.lionsroar.com/thich-nhat-hanh/ or https://thichnhathanhfoundation.org/thich-nhat-hanh
4 *Joanna Macy,* https://www.joannamacy.net/main
5 *Craig Hamilton, Principles of Evolutionary Culture,*
   https://www.openedge.org.uk/uploads/2/6/5/3/26534989/principles_of_a_transformative_culture.pdf
6 *The Bodhisattva Prayer,* this prayer was written by Shantideva, a Buddhist monk of the Mahayana tradition who lived around 700 AD. He was a devoted practitioner who authored the Bodhicaryavatara or Bodhisattva Way of Life.
7 *Dazzlephrenia, A Gallery of Thought on Consciousness, Awe for Mother Nature, and Wonderment over the Dazzling Cosmos,* Woods Eliot, 2006
8 *David Attenborough,*
   https://www.nationalgeographic.com/travel/article/david-attenborough-series-watch
9 *Iceberg,* From *That Same Old Dance of Seasons,* Rose Diamond, 1986

10 *Invocation – Calling the Whole New Human,* from *Songs of Awakening,* Rose Diamond 2012

11 The final lines are a beautiful Maori song written by Professor Morvin Te Anatipa Simon. https://www.youtube.com/watch?v=K70w32j-n3g

About the Author

Over a lifetime, Rose Diamond has used writing as a transformational tool to explore the inner experience of being an awakening soul here on Earth to have a human experience. She combines the sensibility of a poet with the passion of a whole-person educator and the informed curiosity of a gestalt therapist as she brings the light of awareness to the experience of deep grief. What begins as a means to companion herself through her brother's death, becomes a quest to liberate grief from the control of a culture that has forgotten the sacred, so that it may deliver its gifts of compassion, empowerment and service to life.

Rose is committed to personal and global transformation through the evolution of consciousness and the ensouling of our world. She invites you to participate in the process of soul embodiment by living your own inquiries and discovering your own authentic truths. A Story of Transformation is her fifth published book and she is also the creator of The Sitting with Death and Choosing Life Programme. She lives in Wales and you can find her here:

https://www.sittingwithdeathandchoosinglife.com and www.tribeintransition.net

Printed and bound by CPI Group (UK) Ltd, Croydon, CR0 4YY